BEGINNING # BLUES GUITAR

S0-BFC-554

Approved Curriculum

The Complete Electric Blues Guitar Method

Beginning · Intermediate · Mastering

DAVID HAMBURGER

Alfred, the leader in educational publishing, and the National Guitar Workshop, one of America's finest guitar schools, have joined forces to bring you the best, most progressive educational tools possible. We hope you will enjoy this book and encourage you to look for other fine products from Alfred and the National Guitar Workshop.

Acquisition, editorial, music typesetting, interior design: Nathaniel Gunod, Workshop Arts
Chord and scale illustrations: David Jacobs • Hand illustrations: Barbara Smolover
Recording engineered and produced by Mark Dzuiba, Workshop Sounds, High Falls, New York
Cover photo: Jeff Oshiro • Cover design: Ted Engelbart/Carol Kascsak
Cover model: David White • Guitar courtesy of Fender Musical Instruments Corp.

NATIONAL GUITAR WORKSHOP   Alfred

TABLE OF CONTENTS

ABOUT THE AUTHOR

Boston-born David Hamburger now lives in Brooklyn, New York. He teaches privately in New York and is on the faculty of the National Guitar Summer Workshop, where he has co-led blues guitar seminars with Gatemouth Brown, Ronnie Earl and Tinsley Ellis. David divides his time between his own solo and band work as guitarist/songwriter, and doing live and session work on guitar, pedal steel and dobro. He has played on over a dozen independent recordings and released his own album, *King of the Brooklyn Delta.*

INTRODUCTION

This book is the result of years of private and classroom teaching and many more years of listening to, playing and learning about the blues and blues guitar. The blues is known as a "feel" music, something you can't learn about from a book or in a class. It is true that the real nuances, the finesse, the emotion, of any style of music all defy the printed page. And the intuition essential to the mastery of any art form is not something learned in an afternoon. However, the blues has a history of knowledge being passed around from one person to another. Every well-know musician interviewed, it seems, can recall quite precisely who gave them their first guitar, who showed them their first licks, what records they heard and who they saw play when they were first starting-out.

With that in mind, this book is designed to give you plenty of hands-on material to practice and play. Rhythm guitar, soloing, various styles of the blues and concepts of improvising are covered in detail. There are exercises to develop the left hand techniques such as bending and vibrato, and full chorus examples of everything from the Texas and Chicago styles of rhythm guitar to soloing with call-and-response using the pentatonic scales.

The blues is a language, and this book can teach you some of the important vocabulary. To become fluent in the language, however, you will need to listen to many recordings, go hear lots of live music, and play with as many people as possible.

ACKNOWLEDMENTS

I would like to thank the following people for making this book possible: my students, past and present, Jeff Wyman, Fats Kaplin, Stacey Phillips, George Mechem, Stedman Hinckley, Bill Barron, Carlo Rotella, John Good, Victoria Haughey, Joe Sokol, Robert Sherman, Aliyah Baruchin, Leslie Spitz-Edson, Peter Wallach, Andy Resnick, Colin Aberdeen, Michelle Johnson, David and Barbara Smolover, Gary Klein, Jeff McErlain, Pat Bergeson, Paul Yutzy, Paul Howard, Ed Russell, Peter Einhorn, Nat Gunod, Mark Dziuba, Gail Greenberg, Finally, and above all, my patient and supportive family.

000

Track
00.0

An audio recording is available for every book in this series. We hope it will make learning with these books easier and more enjoyable. This symbol will appear next to every example that is played on the audio recording. Use the recording— and your rewind button!— to help insure that you are capturing the feel of each example, interpreting the rhythms correctly, and so on. If you have the compact disc version of this book, you can use the Track numbers below the symbol to go directly to the examples for any page. Have fun!

CHAPTER 1

Getting Started

If the word "theory" makes you run screaming at the thought of billions of weird scales, zillions of useless chords and humorless musicians with slide rules and calculators slowly sucking all the fun out of playing the guitar, consider this:

If you know that a G chord is called a G chord, you know some theory. If you've ever counted off a song, even to yourself, by saying, "a-one, two, three, *and-*", you know some theory. If you can tell the difference between the low string and the high string on the guitar, you know some theory. The way chords are named, the number of beats in bar, whether one note is higher or lower than another one—that's what theory is all about. Theory is just a way of using words and numbers to describe music.

Understanding everything in this chapter completely and immediately is not essential. Some ideas won't start to click until you get into playing the material in the book and see for yourself how things work on the guitar. Then you may want to refer back here to read more about a concept. Try and read through this whole chapter first and get an idea of what's covered. Besides, you never know, some of it might actually make sense!

HALF STEPS, WHOLE STEPS, AND THE IMPORTANCE OF GRAVITY

There are a few things in the world of music that just defy explanation. It's like gravity; we all live with it every day, but very few of us are actually able to explain why, when you knock a bowl of Oreos off the kitchen table, it crashes on the floor, not the ceiling.

Our introduction to music begins with just this sort of situation.

The smallest distance you can travel on one string on the guitar is one fret. "One fret" is a physical unit of measurement. You can see it when you move from, say, the second fret to the third fret.

The musical term for this distance is a *half step*. A half step is the smallest distance you can travel between two notes in western music.

A distance of two frets is called a *whole step*. For example, the distance from the third fret to the fifth fret is a whole step. Half steps and whole steps are the basic building blocks of music.

I hear you say, "But *why* is one fret a half step? Why is a half step as small as you can get?"

This is where the Oreos come in. Because the answer is, "It just *is*." Some of the most basic rules in music theory seem as arbitrary and unreasonable as gravity, but they've been in place for so long that there is nothing you can do but acknowledge them and move on. Or risk wasting a great deal of time, energy and cookies.

THE FRETBOARD

Every note you can play on the guitar—at any fret on any string—has a name. The *open strings* from low to high are: **E   A   D   G   B   E**

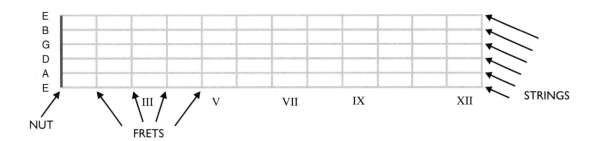

As you go up the neck, climbing fret by fret, the letters go up. But some letters are a whole step (two frets) apart and some are only a half step (one fret) apart.

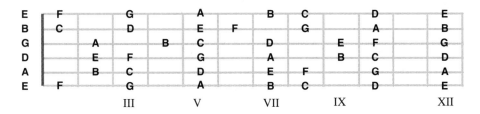

It's not symmetrical but it is consistent: the half-steps are always between B and C, and between E and F.

This still leaves some blank, unnamed frets on the fingerboard. These are filled in by *sharp* and *flat* notes. A sharp ♯ raises a note a half step. For example, D♯ lies between D and E. A flat ♭ lowers a note a half step: D♭ lies between D and C. A *double flat* ♭♭ lowers a note a whole step, and a *double sharp* ✕ raises a note by a whole step. Here's the whole fingerboard laid out with all the notes:

		F	F♯/G♭	G	G♯/A♭	A	A♯/B♭	B	C	C♯/D♭	D	D♯/E♭	E
E		F	F♯/G♭	G	G♯/A♭	A	A♯/B♭	B	C	C♯/D♭	D	D♯/E♭	E
B		C	C♯/D♭	D	D♯/E♭	E	F	F♯/G♭	G	G♯/A♭	A	A♯/B♭	B
G		G♯/A♭	A	A♯/B♭	B	C	C♯/D♭	D	D♯/E♭	E	F	F♯/G♭	G
D		D♯/E♭	E	F	F♯/G♭	G	G♯/A♭	A	A♯/B♭	B	C	C♯/D♭	D
A		A♯/B♭	B	C	C♯/D♭	D	D♯/E♭	E	F	F♯/G♭	G	G♯/A♭	A
E		F	F♯/G♭	G	G♯/A♭	A	A♯/B♭	B	C	C♯/D♭	D	D♯/E♭	E
			III		V		VII		IX			XII	

Yes, it's true, a note can have more than one name, like D♯ and E♭. Impress your friends and foil your enemies by referring to such notes as *enharmonic equivalents*: notes that sound the same but have different names. You will also need to know about the *natural* sign ♮ which cancels out an accidental previously added to a note.

To tune your guitar, place your finger at the fifth fret of the low E string, and raise or lower the A string until the pitches sound the same. Continue this procedure for all the strings, but notice that you fret the G string at the *fourth* fret to tune the B string.

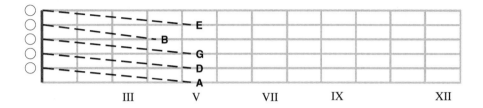

This will work best if you first tune your low E to something constant and unchanging, like a piano, keyboard, pitch pipe, harmonica or a tuning fork.

MUSIC NOTATION

PITCH

Music notation is a way of graphing notes—their *pitches* and *time values*, or *rhythms*—so that they can be understood by a guitarist or any other musician.

Music is represented by the *staff*. The staff has five lines.

1

The symbol at the beginning is called a *G clef*. One end of the G clef curls around to rest on the line used to show the note G.

Each line or space represents a letter from the same musical alphabet we have on the guitar fingerboard. The bottom line is the same E that we have at the fourth string, second fret. The top line is the same F as the first fret on the first string.

2

Pitches are shown by placing *note heads* on the lines or in the spaces. When sharp, flat and natural symbols are needed they are placed *before* the note heads. Here are the notes on the staff from E up to F and back, using sharps on the way up and flats on the way back down.

3

Ledger lines, just long enough to fit a note on, show the notes above and below the range of the staff.

4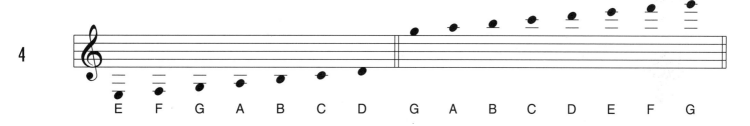

We have enough notation now to show where all the guitar's open strings lie on the staff.

5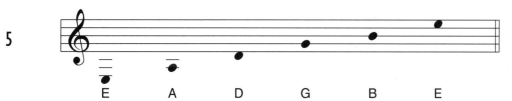

These notes can of course be remembered with the phrase made famous during the sessions for Eric Clapton and Duane Allman's masterpiece "Layla:"

"Eric   And   Duane   Got   the   Blues   Early"

RHYTHM

Notes are grouped together into units called *measures*, which are indicated on the staff by vertical lines called *bar lines*. The end of a song is marked with a *double bar*.

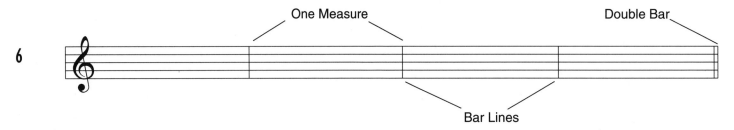

The longest commonly used note length is a *whole note*, which lasts for four *beats*, or the time it takes you to count, "one and two and three and four and." One *half note* is half as long, two beats, or the time it takes you to count, "one and two and." One *quarter note*, the basic unit of counting in music, is one quarter as long as a whole note, or just the time it takes to count "one and."

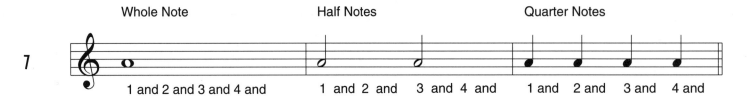

Eighth notes are half as long as quarter notes, just the "one" of "one and." They can be shown several different ways. *Stems* with *flags* are used for individual eighth notes, while connecting *beams* are used for two or more eighth notes.

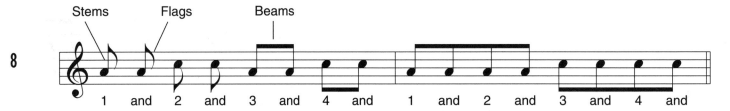

You can think of four *sixteenth notes* to a quarter note instead of counting sixteen notes to the bar. Some people count these as "one-ee-and-ah two-ee-and-ah three-ee-and-ah four-ee-and-ah", which means you probably shouldn't try to count sixteenth notes with peanuts or marbles in your mouth. Sixteenth notes look like eighth notes with all the flags or beams done as double lines.

So here's the big tree of note values, showing how everything breaks down to fit into the same amount of space (four beats or one measure) in different ways:

Note Values

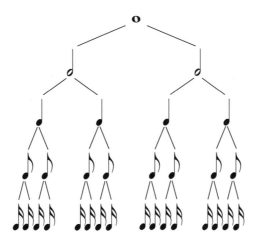

TIME SIGNATURES

Most blues music has four *beats* per measure, which is shown by the *time signature* at the beginning of the staff. The top number tells how many beats there are in one measure, and the bottom number tells what kind of note counts as one beat. In 4/4 time, a quarter note, "one and," counts as one beat.

4 = Four beats per measure
4 = A quarter note receives one beat

Some blues music is counted in *12/8* time. An *eighth* note counts as one beat, and there are twelve of them in a measure. The eighth notes are played in groups of three, so it really sounds like 4/4 time with every beat divided in three.

TIES

A tie attaches one note to another, so that the second of the two is not picked. Rather, its value is added to that of the first.

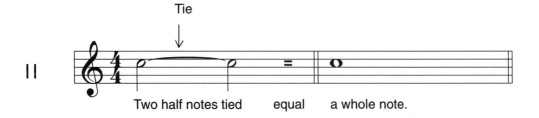

DOTTED NOTES
Or, Let's Hide Away and Study Fractions with Freddie King

A dotted note lasts one and a half times as long as the original undotted version. For example: A whole note lasts for four beats, so a dotted whole note lasts for six beats— a whole note plus a half note. A dotted half note is a half note plus a quarter note. A dotted quarter note is a quarter note plus an eighth note. And a dotted eighth note is an eighth note plus a sixteenth note.

RESTS

Any time you *don't* play needs to be notated too. For every note length, there's a corresponding rest symbol that means "Don't play, for exactly this long, alright?" Here's what they look like:

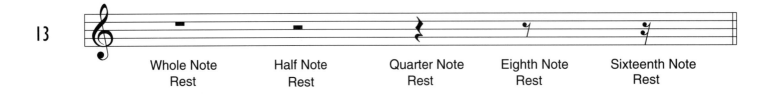

| Whole Note Rest | Half Note Rest | Quarter Note Rest | Eighth Note Rest | Sixteenth Note Rest |

TRIPLETS

Triplets are a way of breaking down a beat into three equal parts instead of two. One beat ordinarily breaks down into two eighth notes, which you count out as "one and;" if you break down one beat into *triplets*, you use eighth notes with a little "3" over or under the beam, and count like this:

1 and ah   2 and ah   3 and ah   4 and ah

If this sort of thing embarasses you, you could also just count it "*one* two three, *two* two three, *three* two three, *four* two three."

SWING EIGHTHS

If you take triplet eighth notes and tie together the first two notes of each set of three, the result is called *swing eighths*—the essential shuffle rhythm used throughout the blues:

15

This rhythm is so common in blues and jazz that it has its own name and notational shorthand. Swing eighths are written as regular looking eighth notes on the page. But whenever you see any of the following at the top of the page, at the beginning of an example, on the sheet music, etc.....

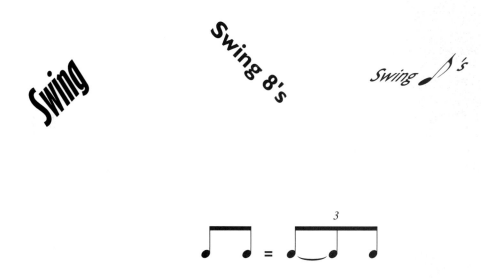

....it means you should play all the eighth notes as if they were like those tied sets of triplets. In this book, all examples are assumed to be in swing eighths unless specifically marked "*straight eighths*."

READING TABLATURE

Tablature is a purely graphic way of showing what to play on the guitar. There are six lines, each representing one of the strings. Numbers placed on the lines indicate what fret to play on that string.

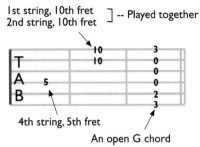

1st string, 10th fret
2nd string, 10th fret] -- Played together

4th string, 5th fret

An open G chord

When tablature is used alone, standard rhythmic notation can be used—bar lines, time signatures, beams and stems for various note values, and rest symbols. In this book, the tablature is always written parallel to the standard notation, which already contains all the rhythmic information, so the tablature only indicates the fret numbers and strings. If you suspect that this is a conspiracy on the part of the publisher, the editor, the author, and a cynical consortium of ecologically unsound yet wily and unstoppable multinational corporations to encourage you to work on reading the standard notation instead of relying on just the tab, you're only partly right.

READING CHORD BOXES

Chord boxes show a portion of the guitar neck, with the strings represented by vertical lines and the frets represented by horizontal lines. The numbers across the top show the left hand fingers to use (see the picture of the hand below), the numbers along the bottom tell what note of the chord (root, fifth, etc.) is being played on which string. An "x" is an unplayed or muted note, an "o" is an open string. A Roman numeral on the right helps you find the correct fret for the chord. When one finger plays more than one string (bar chords) it is shown with a bar crossing all the strings covered by that finger.

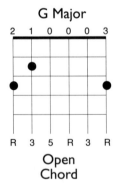

G Major

Open
Chord

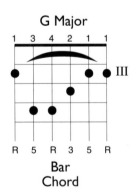

G Major

Bar
Chord

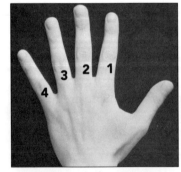

*The fingers of the left hand
are numbered.*

READING A CHORD CHART— RHYTHMIC NOTATION

A chord chart tells you what chords and rhythms to play. It gives you chord names and assumes you know at least one way to play each of those chords. The rhythms are indicated with standard bar lines and rhythmic notation. Each chord is represented by one or more slashes:

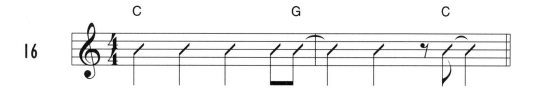

You will see chord charts throughout this book. Also, many of the melodic examples have chord symbols written above the music. Playing along with the tape available for this book, or taping yourself playing the chords and then playing the example along with the tape will help you get a better idea of how the lick is meant to be used. Or, even better, you could trade off with another guitarist (or even your teacher). Guitar players are often given just a chord progression and asked to create their own rhythm parts. Try and apply what you learn about rhythm guitar to the chords in the examples throughout the book.

READING SCALE DIAGRAMS

There are many scales and patterns introduced in this book. Like the chord boxes, the scale diagrams illustrate a section of the neck. In the scale diagram the strings are horizontal lines and the frets are represented by vertical lines.

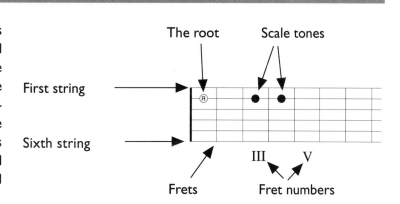

READING ROMAN NUMERALS

Okay, scholars, here's a review of Roman numerals and their Arabic equivalents:

I	1	IV	4	VII	7	X	10	XIII	13	XVI	16
II	2	V	5	VIII	8	XI	11	XIV	14	XVII	17
III	3	VI	6	IX	9	XII	12	XV	15		

CHAPTER 2

Blues Theory

If you understand half and whole steps, note names and sharps and flats, you know enough to understand how scales, chords, keys and harmony work—everything you need to know to understand what's in this book.

THE MAJOR SCALE

Our basic reference point is the *major scale,* which is the scale you get when you sing "do, re, mi, fa, so, la, ti, do." Here's a C Major scale ("do" is C):

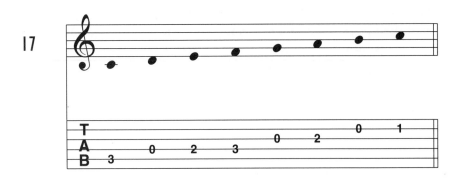

17

Notice where the whole steps and half steps fall in this scale. This pattern is the definition of a major scale.

Notes:	C	D	E	F	G	A	B	C
Steps:		W	W	H	W	W	W	H

W = whole step
H = half step

SCALE DEGREES

The notes of the scale are numbered according to their distance from the first note, which is called the *root* (R). In the C Major scale, D is the *second degree* of the scale, or 2nd, E is the 3rd, and so on. The scale degrees are written above the staff in this example.

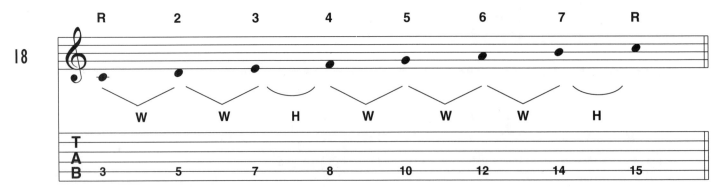

18

Using sharps and flats, it is possible to create a major scale from any note.

The Major Scales

1	2	3	4	5	6	7	8
C	D	E	F	G	A	B	C
G	A	B	C	D	E	F♯	G
D	E	F♯	G	A	B	C♯	D
A	B	C♯	D	E	F♯	G♯	A
E	F♯	G♯	A	B	C♯	D♯	E
B	C♯	D♯	E	F♯	G♯	A♯	B
F♯	G♯	A♯	B	C♯	D♯	E♯	F♯
G♭	A♭	B♭	C♭	D♭	E♭	F	G♭
D♭	E♭	F	G♭	A♭	B♭	C	D♭
A♭	B♭	C	D♭	E♭	F	G	A♭
E♭	F	G	A♭	B♭	C	D	E♭
B♭	C	D	E♭	F	G	A	B♭
F	G	A	B♭	C	D	E	F

} Enharmonic*

*The F♯ and G♭ scales are actually all the same notes (enharmonically equivalent), so, including C Major, there are a total of twelve major scales.

KEY SIGNATURES

A key signature is a collection of all the flats or sharps that are used in a particular scale. It is placed at the beginning of a line of music to indicate what notes should always be sharped or flatted in that music, creating the sound of a particular *key*. For example, if you always sharp C and F, it will create an overall sound of the D Major scale, or the key of D.

The Twelve Key Signatures

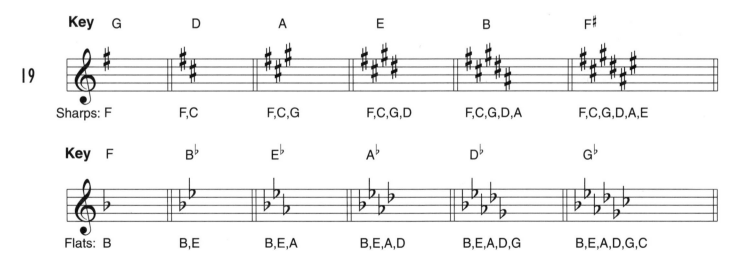

Sharps and flats take their names from the line or space on which they appear. Since a note on the top line of the staff would be an F, for instance, a sharp on that line would be an F sharp.

Minor scales are derived from major scales. For example, A Minor is made up of the notes of the C Major scale, played from A to A.

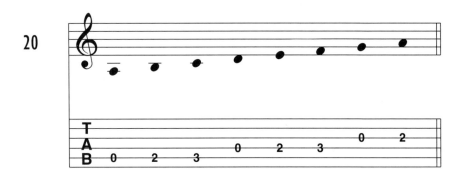

The minor scale, like the major scale, has a formula of whole steps and half steps, making it possible to create a minor scale starting from any note.

Notes:	A		B		C		D		E		F		G		A
Steps:		W		H		W		W		H		W		W	

W = whole step
H = half step

Compared to an A Major scale, the 3rd, 6th and 7th degrees of A Minor are all a half step closer to the root of the scale. These degrees are said to be *flatted* or *minor* and are indicated with a flat sign.

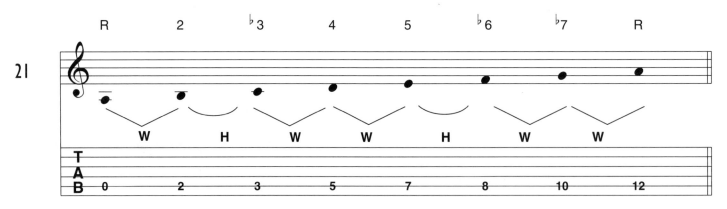

RELATIVE MINOR

Every relative minor scale has the same notes and the same key signature as its relative major scale, and always begins and ends on the sixth degree of the relative major scale. Because it is directly related to the C Major scale, A Minor is called the *relative minor* scale of C Major. C Major is called the *relative major* of A Minor. There is a relative minor scale for every one of the twelve major scales.

Key Signature	Major Key	Minor Key
	C	A
	G	E
	D	B
	A	F#
	E	C#
	B	G#
	F#	D#

Key Signature	Major Key	Minor Key
	F	D
	B♭	G
	E♭	C
	A♭	F
	D♭	B♭
	G♭	E♭

The relative minor scale is called *natural minor* because it contains no alterations (no additional sharps or flats beyond those indicated in the key signature). There are several different kinds of minor scales, but throughout this book the term *minor scale* will always refer to the natural minor scale.

Magic Sam

INTERVALS

An interval is the distance between two notes. We have already been using intervals to build scales and measure scale degrees. Our basic unit of measurement, the half step, is also called a *minor second*. We have been using *major seconds*, or whole steps, (one half step larger than a minor second), major and minor 3rds, 6ths and 7ths, and perfect 4ths, 5ths and octaves to measure distances from the root to the various degrees of the scale.

A perfect or major interval that has been increased by a half step is called *augmented*. A perfect interval that has been decreased by a half step is called *diminished*. It is helpful to measure all intervals in half steps.

Half steps	Pitches	Interval	
0	C - C	unison	
1	C - C♯	augmented unison	} Enharmonic
1	C - D♭	minor 2nd	
2	C - D	major 2nd	
3	C - D♯	augmented 2nd	} Enharmonic
3	C - E♭	minor 3rd	
4	C - E	major 3rd	
5	C - F	perfect 4th	
6	C - F♯	augmented 4th	} Enharmonic
6	C - G♭	diminished 5th	
7	C - G	perfect 5th	
8	C - G♯	augmented 5th	} Enharmonic
8	C - A♭	minor 6th	
9	C - A	major 6th	
10	C - A♯	augmented 6th	} Enharmonic
10	C - B♭	minor 7th	
11	C - B	major 7th	
12	C - C	perfect octave	

Here is a sample of some intervals in standard notation and TAB.

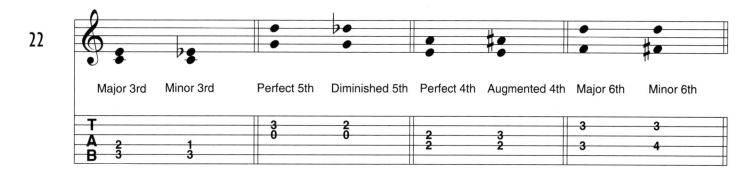

CHORDS

A chord is two or more notes played together. All chords can be built on any note, just like scales. We will deal with five kinds of chords in this book: *major, minor, dominant 7th, dominant 9th, minor 7th, diminished* and *augmented*.

Major chords are built from the root, major 3rd and perfect 5th of a major scale (R, 3, 5). The three notes that create a chord are called a *triad*.

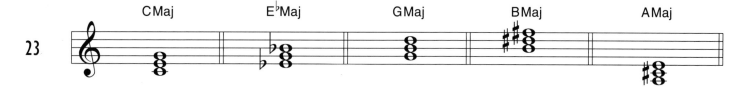

Minor chords are built from the root, minor 3rd (or $\flat$3) and perfect 5th of a minor scale (R, $\flat$3, 5). You can build a minor triad from any note.

An augmented triad is a major triad with an augmented 5th, or $\sharp$5 (R, 3, $\sharp$5).

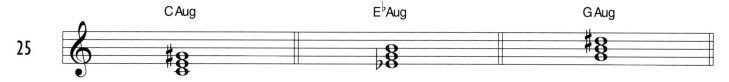

A diminished triad is a minor triad with a diminished 5th, or $\flat$5 (R, $\flat$3, $\flat$5).

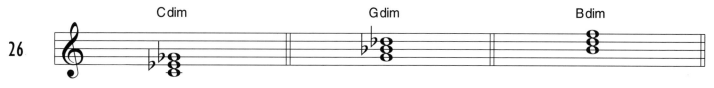

A dominant 7th chord, usually referred to as a "7th" chord, is a major triad with a minor 7th ($^\flat$7) added (R, 3, 5, $^\flat$7).

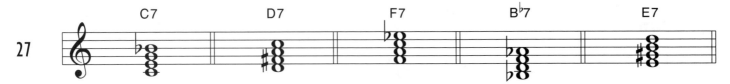

A minor 7th chord is a minor triad with a minor 7th added (R, $^\flat$3, 5, $^\flat$7).

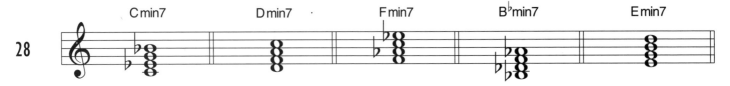

When a 2nd is added to a chord which already has a 7th, that note is called the *9th* of the chord (a 9th is an octave higher than a 2nd).

A dominant 9th chord is a dominant 7th chord with a 9th (2nd) added (R, 3, 5, $^\flat$7, 9).

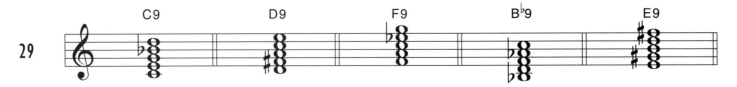

There are three other kinds of chords with 7ths added: *major 7th* chords, *half diminished* chords ($^\varnothing$) and *diminished 7th* ($^\circ$) chords. A major 7th chord is a major triad with a major 7th added (R, 3, 5, 7). A half diminished chord is a diminished triad with a minor 7th added (R, $^\flat$3, $^\flat$5, $^\flat$7). It is often refered to as a minor 7th $^\flat$5 chord (min7$^\flat$5), since it is the same as a minor 7th chord with a lowered 5th. A diminished 7th chord is a diminished triad with a diminished 7th added, which is a 7th that has been lowered by two half steps, (R, $^\flat$3, $^\flat$5, $^{\flat\flat}$7).

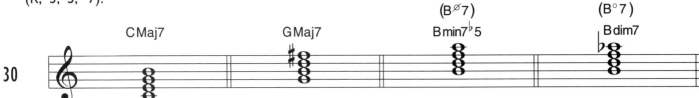

Every key has its own set of chords, one chord for every note of the scale. Each of these chords is built by stacking notes in 3rds using only notes from the key of C Major (using the C Major scale). Since every major scale follows the same formula, every key will have the same sequence of major, minor and diminished chords. These chords can therefore be numbered just like the degrees of the scale. Upper case Roman numerals indicate major chords, lower case Roman numerals indicate minor chords, and a ° indicates a diminished chord.

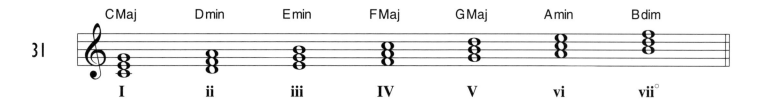

Impress your friends and bandmates by pointing out, for example, that the chords C Major, D Minor, A Minor and G Major are all " *diatonic* to the key of C." When they ask (and they surely will) just what you're talking about, explain that diatonic is a Greek word which basically means "all in one key." Roll your eyes as you do so, implying that you really don't have time to waste with people who lack a thorough background in Greco-Roman linguistics.

It is possible to build 7th chords on every note of the scale as well. The chords are then named by their 7th chord type and root, using Roman numerals and the abbreviations "Maj7" for major 7th, "min7" for minor 7th, "7" for dominant 7th and "min7♭5" for half diminished.

I Maj7   ii min7   iii min7   IV Maj7   V7   vi min7   vii min7♭5

BLUES HARMONY

Guess what—half of this goes out the window as soon as you begin to play the blues. But it's important to know how the blues differs from classical music. Classical music is based on this diatonic harmony, where the I, IV and V chords are major and the only dominant 7th chord in a key is on the V chord. However, in the blues, *every* major chord can be a dominant 7th chord (the I, the IV *and* the V). The basic twelve-bar blues progression is usually composed entirely of 7th chords. The slashes in the music represent the four beats of each measure, although you can strum any blues rhythm you like.

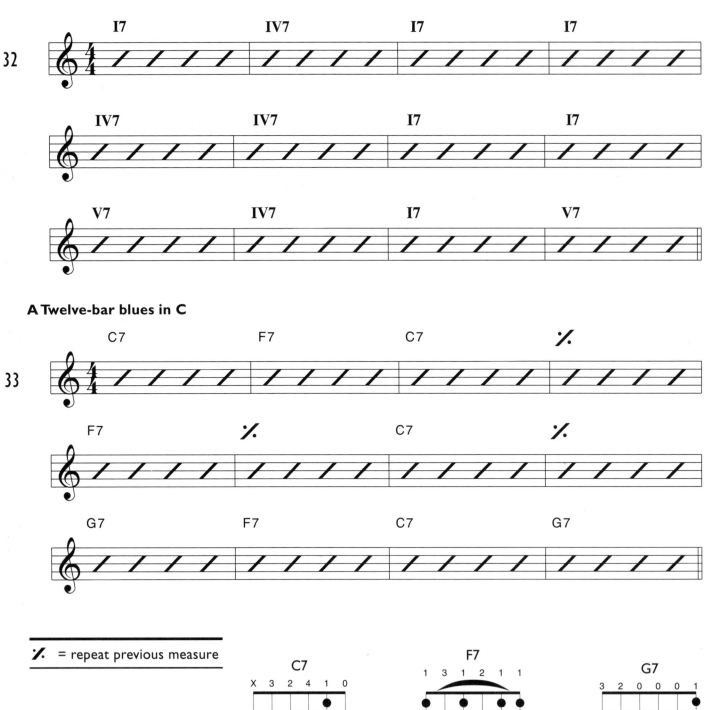

A Twelve-bar blues in C

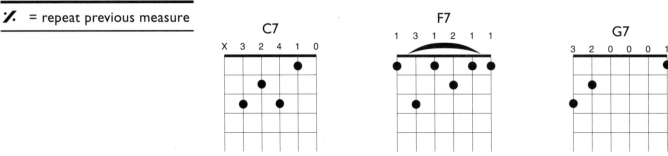

% = repeat previous measure

MINOR BLUES HARMONY

In a minor key, blues harmony is more like classical diatonic harmony. These are the diatonic chords for a minor key. Notice the flat chords (♭III, ♭VI, and ♭VII). The flat tells us that the root of this chord is one half step lower than it would be in a major key.

i   ii°   ♭III   iv   v   ♭VI   ♭VII

For example, here are the diatonic chords in the key of A Minor:

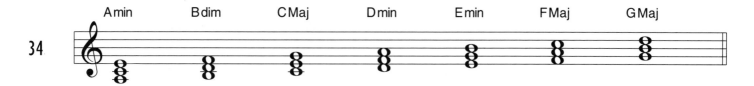

Many minor blues tunes are simply i, iv and v.

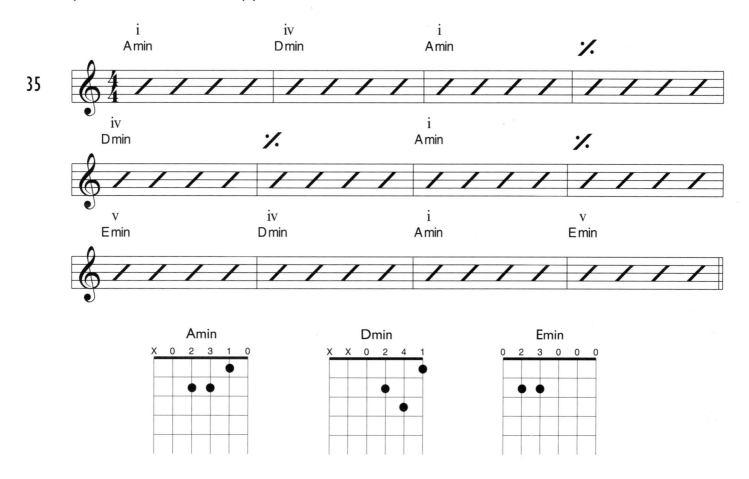

However, the following chords are often included as *substitutes*—chords which are *not* diatonic to the key at all, but sound good anyway:

IV7 can substitute for iv
♭VI can substitute for iv
V7 can substitute for v

CHAPTER 3

Basic Rhythm Guitar

BASIC RHYTHM VOCABULARY

A *voicing* is a specific arrangement of the notes in a particular chord. A *fingering* is a particular way of playing a voicing on the guitar. An *open chord* is one that includes one or more open strings in its fingering. A *bar chord* is one in which all the strings played are fretted by the left hand.

Three important open chord voicings

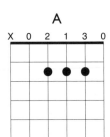

A

X 0 2 1 3 0

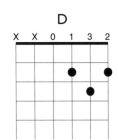

D

X X 0 1 3 2

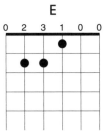

E

0 2 3 1 0 0

Two common bar chord voicings. Bar chords are *moveable* to any fret.

Major, Root on the Sixth String

1 3 4 2 1 1

Root ⟶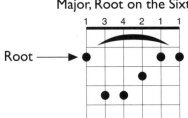

Major, Root on the Fifth String

X 1 3 3 3 X

Root ⟶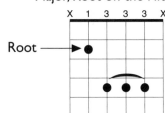

While it is a good idea to practice playing the complete chord, you almost always can get away with only playing the bottom two notes.

OPEN POSITION

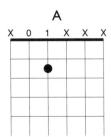

A

X 0 1 X X X

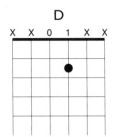

D

X X 0 1 X X

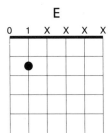

E

0 1 X X X X

CLOSED POSITION

These voicings contain no open strings, so they are moveable to any fret, just like the full bar chords.

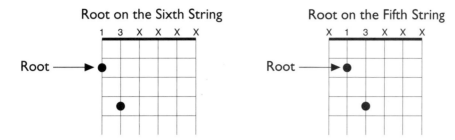

A *chord progression* is a series of chords that lasts a set number of bars, and can be repeated as long as necessary. A *chorus* is one time through a chord progression.

Muddy Waters

As you know by now, a *twelve-bar blues* is a specific chord progression that can be played in any key. Here is one chorus of a twelve-bar blues in the key of A, showing a very basic rhythm guitar part. Remember to swing the eighths!

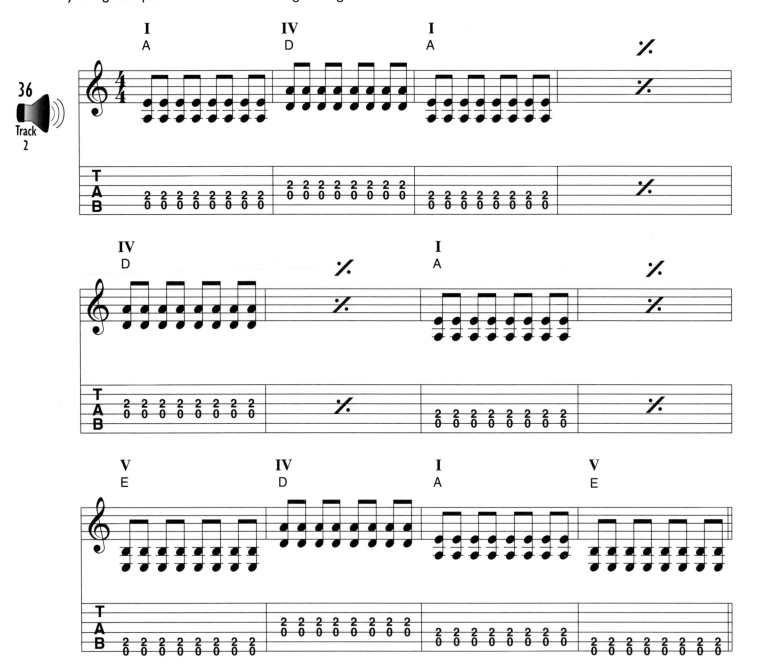

Literally thousands of songs have been created using the twelve-bar blues form. There may be subtle variations on the chords, the rhythm, the tempo and the feel within this structure, but the basic idea remains the same. The most common variations are to leave out the IV7 chord in the second measure, or the V7 in the last measure, or both.

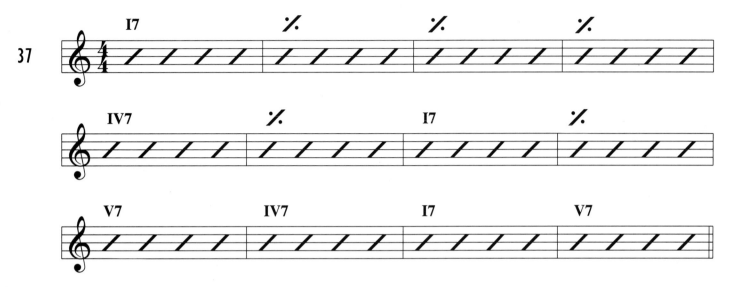

Another possibility, found in swing and boogie-woogie styles, is to start the *turnaround* (last four measures, see Chapter 7 for a complete study of the turnaround) with a iimin7 chord, go to the V7 chord, and return to I7, skipping the IV7.

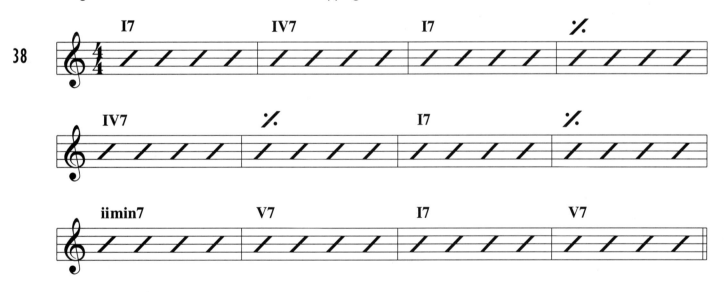

PALM MUTING

This is an important part of creating a good sound. Rest the fleshy part of your right hand palm lightly where the low strings meet the bridge of the guitar. If it sounds completely muted, move your hand closer to the bridge. If it sounds no different than regular strumming, move your hand further from the bridge. When you pick with all downstrokes, you should get a chunky sound that doesn't sustain for too long.

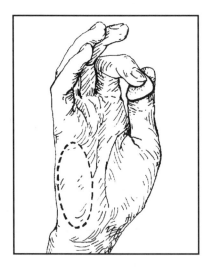

Use this part of your hand to mute.

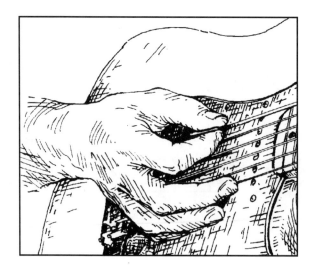

Rest your palm lightly by the bridge.

THE SHUFFLE PATTERN

Somewhere in between a chord and a riff, the guitar shuffle pattern is as old as Robert Johnson, and just as cool. Use palm muting and use your third finger to play the notes on the fourth fret.

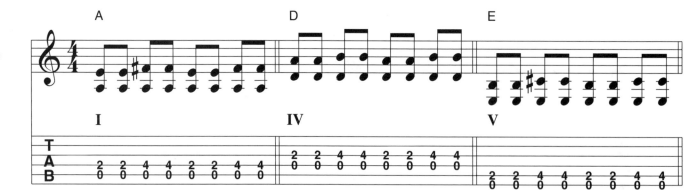

Here is another twelve-bar blues in the key of A, this time using the shuffle pattern. Notice the break in the pattern in the last bar. The eighth-note rest means you begin playing in the last bar on the "and of one."

Using moveable bar chords lets you play shuffle patterns in any key. For example, using the moveable two-note versions of the bar chords given on page 27, here are the three chords for playing a blues in the key of G, voiced with the roots on the sixth string. Remember, the Roman numerals will help you find the right frets.

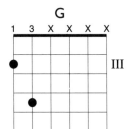

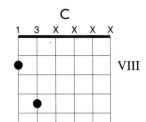

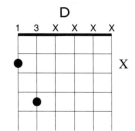

Here are the same chords, voiced with the roots on the fifth string.

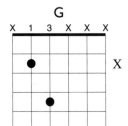

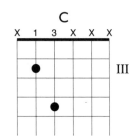

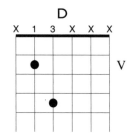

Stretch with your fourth finger to create the shuffle pattern with the moveable bar chords.

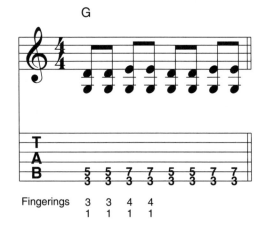

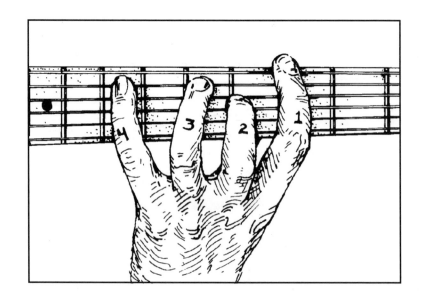

Left hand muting is done by releasing the pressure on the note, immediately after you play it, but keeping your finger on the string so that it is dampened. This makes the note shorter than notated, or *staccato*.

Blues in G with bar chords
Using a combination of voicings with roots on the sixth string and roots on the fifth string means you don't have to jump around the fretboard as much. Here is a twelve-bar blues in G using the shuffle pattern and chords that stay within four frets. Use left hand muting on the first of each pair of eighth notes.

Here are some variations on the basic shuffle pattern, shown on a moveable C chord.

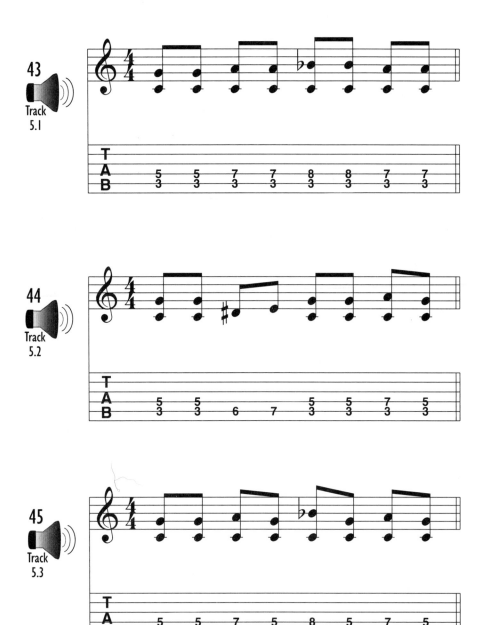

Stop time means the whole band plays together on a series of rhythmic figures, called *hits*, within the framework of a regular chord progression. This example combines bar chord fingerings with open strings. Pay close attention to the rhythm.

This example begins with a *pickup*. The first three eighth notes start on the "and of three." You should count "one and two and three" and then begin. Songs with pickups can have *incomplete measures* at the end. The incomplete measure is missing that portion of the measure that was used for the pickup. The incomplete measure at the end is usually overlooked in the blues.

The key of E is a favorite for guitar players because of all the possibilities with the low, ringing open E and A strings. Here's a chorus of blues in E in the boogie-woogie style. Boogie-woogie is a more rolling, open-feeling cousin of the shuffle. T-Bone Walker pioneered the boogie-woogie feel for blues guitarists, followed by fellow Southwesterner, Gatemouth Brown, and the influence of this style can be heard even today in the music of the late Stevie Ray Vaughn, who fused boogie-woogie bass lines with a solid Texas shuffle feel on tunes like "Pride and Joy" and "I'm Cryin'." Play without any palm muting and use *alternate picking*. In alternate picking, we move the pick down-up-down-up, etc.

The B Major chord is V in the key of E, so you'll need to choose a voicing for that chord. Use either of the bar chord voicings on page 26, using a B as the root note on either the fifth or sixth string, depending on the voicing you choose.

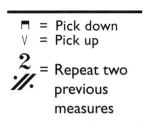

⊓ = Pick down
V = Pick up

= Repeat two previous measures

CHAPTER 4

Blues Scales

Blues scales are *what* you play. Phrasing, timing, feel and style are *how* you play. The two most common blues scales are the major and minor pentatonic scales. It is important to get a solid grasp on what notes are in each scale and how to finger them quickly and accurately on the guitar. It is equally important to begin developing a hands-on sense of how the blues is played, through working on these exercises and listening to how blues players—of all instruments, not just guitar—actually play, how their personality and command of their instrument makes the notes come alive. There are only so many notes in these scales, yet everyone manages to sound different—to sound like themselves. You can too.

MAJOR PENTATONIC

The major pentatonic scale is a five-note scale. It is a major scale with the 4th and the 7th left out.

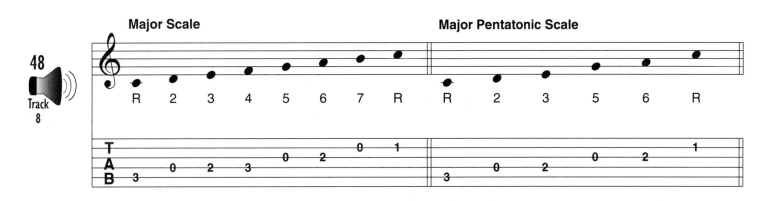

Here is a two-octave fingering for the major pentatonic scale. Because it has no open strings, it can be moved, like a bar chord, to any fret to create a major pentatonic scale in any key. This one is in C, because the roots are C notes.

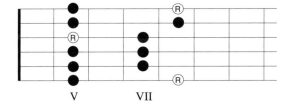

PHRASING

Phrasing is the length and timing of what you play. A musical phrase can be long or short, relaxed or hurried, smooth or disruptive, just like a spoken phrase. Phrases are the smallest unit of improvising—even one note can be a phrase! The phrases below are grouped according to their rhythmic similarities, and all of them center around the root or the 5th of the major pentatonic scale. Notice that many of these examples start with pickups.

CALL-AND-RESPONSE PHRASING

Some of the best blues playing is based on the very simple idea of playing a phrase, then repeating it and adding to it or changing it a little. This is one kind of *call-and-response*. The first phrase is the *call* and the second one is the *response*. Try these examples first, then take some other phrases and create your own responses.

Here are typical voicings for the chords that go with these examples. Notice that they are both *moveable* voicings. The root for the one on the left (F7) is on the sixth string, so all you have to do is move this chord to the fret that has the desired root note on the sixth string. The root for the voicing on the right (C7) is on the fifth string.

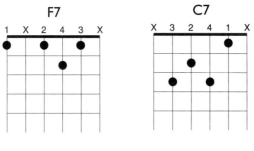

A *riff* is a short, rhythmic phrase strong enough to be the basis for a call-and-response type of solo, but simple enough to be played repeatedly as a *backup* part behind a vocal or another soloist without getting in the way. Here's a twelve-bar riff style chorus in the key of C. When you can play it comfortably, play along with this example on the tape available for this book, or tape the chord progression using one of the shuffle patterns and play the riff part over it. Notice how call-and-response is used to build the solo.

The minor pentatonic scale is also a five-note scale. This one is a minor scale with the 2nd and 6th left out.

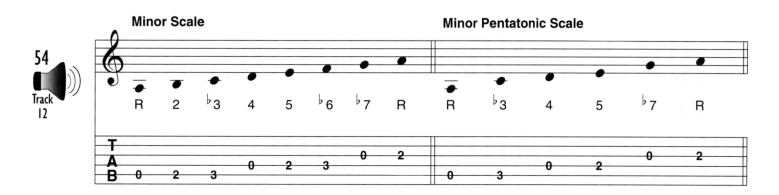

Here is a two-octave fingering for the minor pentatonic scale. Like the major pentatonic scale, it has no open strings and therefore can also be moved to any fret to create a minor pentatonic scale in any key. This one is in A, because all the roots are A notes.

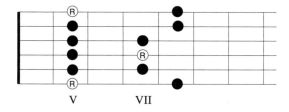

The following chord voicings will come in handy with the upcoming examples.

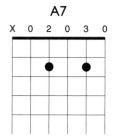
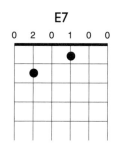
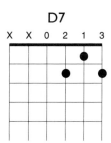

The minor pentatonic scale includes the root notes of all three chords in the standard twelve-bar blues progression. For example, in the key of A, the I, IV and V chords are A, D, and E, and all three of these notes—the roots of those chords—are found in the A Minor pentatonic scale.

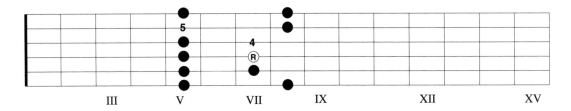

Many blues players *target* the roots of the chords when they play. That is, while they may solo in one scale for the whole chord progression—the scale based on the same root as the I chord—the note on which they choose to end a phrase depends on where they are in the chord progression. For example, in an A blues, play A Minor pentatonic throughout, but end phrases on the note A during the A chords, on the note D during the D chords, and on the note E during the E chords.

Here are a number of phrases, each ended three different ways—once on each of the three roots of an A blues chord progression. For example:

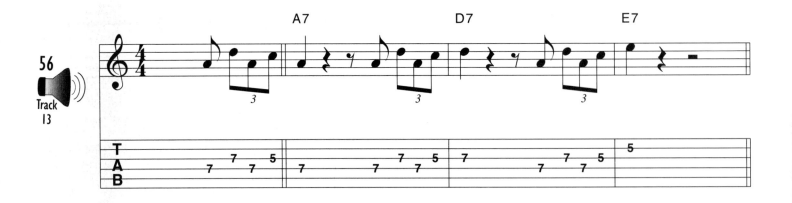

Freddie King

COMBINING CALL-AND-RESPONSE WITH ROOT TARGETING

Here's a chorus of a blues in A that combines the ideas of call-and-response, riff-style phrasing with targeting the roots. This one uses the A Minor pentatonic scale.

Transposing means moving something to another key. This is done because you want to sing a song you know in a higher or lower key, or because you have learned a lick in one key and you want to apply it to a chord progression in a different key, or...or because something like this happens:

> ## "Every Day I Get The (Loft Party Art Crowd) Blues"
>
> You get invited to a loft party in New York City's Soho district. The discreet gold-embossed card clearly requests you to bring your axe (amplification will be provided —hopefully tweed Fenders from the '50s). You arrive fashionably late, mingle with the black-tie crowd, pretend to enjoy the suspicious-looking paté, and gradually make your way over to the bandstand. Suddenly you're hoisted from the crowd to the stage, roadies plug you in, the lights go down, the spotlights go up, and B.B. King steps out from behind the horn section with his 335 and says, "<u>Every Day I Get The Blues,</u> in D♭, baby - you kick it off."

What do you do?

A) Ask around for a capo.

B) Explain that you don't play in D♭—you *used* to, but you don't anymore.

C) Panic, drop your paté on B.B.'s shoes. Realize what you've done. Say, "Oh wow, man, I'm really sorry...Were those expensive?"

D) Find D♭ on the low E string (hint: try the ninth fret). Play in D♭ Minor pentatonic with your first finger at the ninth fret, or, play in D♭ Major pentatonic with your fourth finger at the ninth fret (and your first finger at the sixth fret).

If you picked D, you are on the road to mastering transposing. If you're still confused, just remember: find out what key the song is in, find the root note of that key on the sixth string, and try the major or minor pentatonic scale starting there. (Note: Don't worry about why B.B. King is playing an art opening instead of the Apollo Theater. Stranger things have happened.)

CHAPTER 5

Left Hand Techniques

In this chapter we'll explore the left hand techniques of *hammer-ons*, *pull-offs*, *slides*, *bends*, and *vibrato*. All of these techniques are ways of shaping and coloring phrases.

HAMMER-ONS

To do a hammer-on, fret a note with your left hand (or play an open note), pick it with your right hand, and then place another left hand finger on the same string, making a second note sound without actually picking a second time. This is shown in the music and TAB by a curved line called a *slur*, and a letter "H" in the TAB, between the note picked and the hammered-on note.

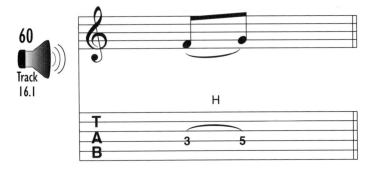

It is important that you bring down the finger for the second note quickly and accurately. While the vibration of the string from the first note is a factor in making the second note sound, it's the way your finger forces the string against the fret as it lands on the second note that matters most. Imagine that you are dropping your fingertip directly to the fretboard, and the string just happens to be in the way.

These exercises ascend and/or descend the G Minor pentatonic scale with hammer-ons.

62
Track 17.1

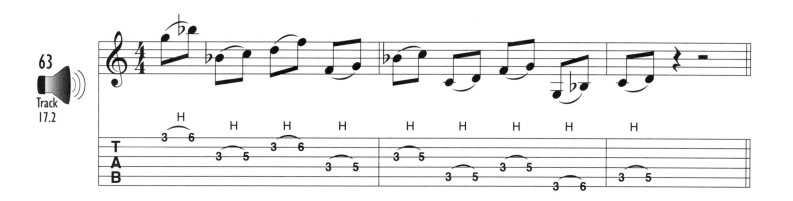

63
Track 17.2

Buddy Guy

PHOTO • INSTITUTE OF JAZZ STUDIES

To do a pull-off, pick a fretted note, then lift off your finger to let another note on the same string (fretted or open) ring out. It's called a pull-off because you actually pluck the string with your left hand finger. The vibration of the string from picking the first note is not as important as the sound you make pulling down and away with your left hand finger. When pulling-off to a fretted note, be sure to put both fingers down together before picking the first note.

This is shown in the music and TAB with a slur, and a letter "P" in the TAB between the note picked and the pulled-off note.

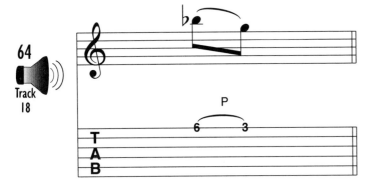

64
Track 18

You can use your left hand fingers to mute the strings you aren't playing. This will help you eliminate extra notes or weird, unwanted noises as you pull-off.

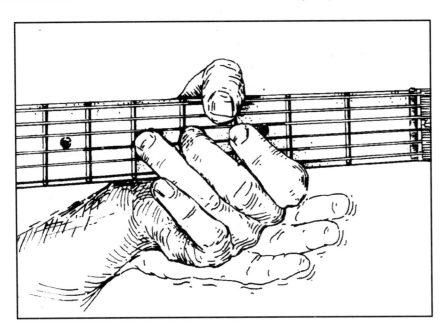

For instance, your first finger can mute the first and second string as your third finger executes a pull-off on the third string. The thumb is also useful for muting the lower strings.

Here are some exercises for pull-offs, once again in G Minor pentatonic.

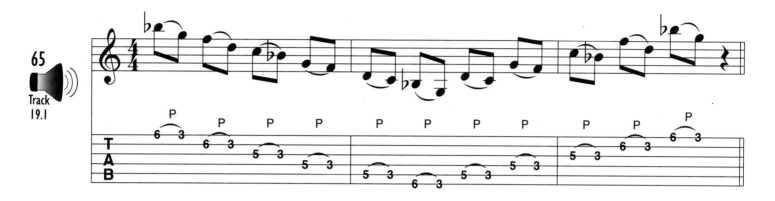

65
Track
19.1

66
Track
19.2

67
Track
19.3

HAMMER-ONS AND PULL-OFFS TOGETHER

Okay, so everyone knows the blues isn't about *speed*, it's that *feel* thing, that *taste* thing, right? Well, this is true, but then again what about Robben Ford? Or Buddy Guy?

"Um, excuse me, Mr. Guy, a few of us were talking and we thought you should know, all those fast licks you play, it kind of undermines your credibility as a blues player and, well, frankly we've noticed that while you've gotten faster and faster over the years, you're playing with less and less feel."

Is this the case? Of course not.

Alright then! Speed is valuable as an option, although not for its own sake. Combining hammer-ons and pull-offs can be used to create a smoother, more fluid sound and yes, by playing more notes with each right hand pick stroke, you can play faster as well. Here are a few exercises to get going. Try to keep the accent on the first and third beats.

⊓ = Pick down
V = Pick up

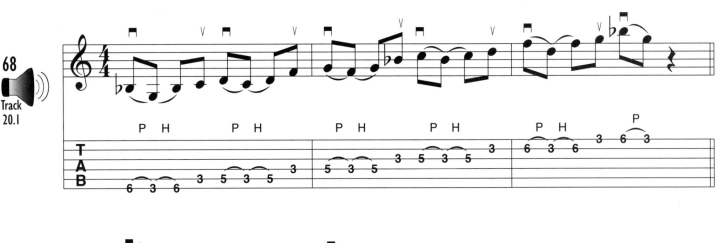

With a little imagination, parts of these exercises can be mysteriously transformed into actual musical ideas.

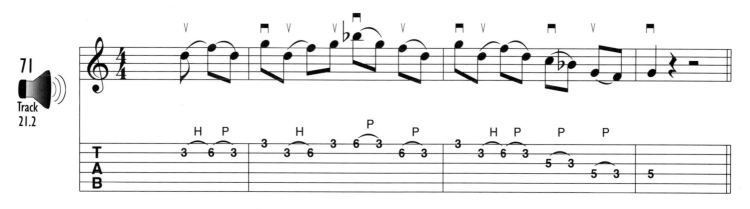

To do a slide, finger a note and pick it, then slide your left hand finger along the string, up or down the fretboard, to a new fret position. Keep enough pressure on the string to keep the string sounding, but not so much that it's difficult to move your hand around.

The notation for a slide in the music and TAB is just a diagonal line leading from the starting note up or down to the note you're meant to slide into, and an "S" in the TAB.

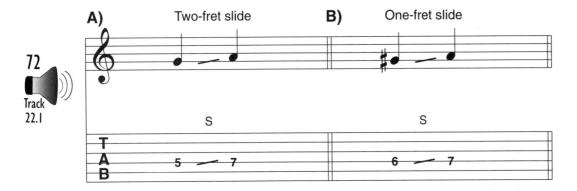

There are two main ways to use slides. One is to begin a phrase by sliding into the starting note. The other is to slide to a note beyond the position you are playing in. Both are largely a matter of taste, so beyond these few examples the experimentation is up to you.

In general, sliding works best with phrases that begin on a downbeat, though any of the short phrases we have been working with could be begun with a slide. Place the finger that would ordinarily play your starting note one or two frets above or below that note on the same string. On the beat where the lick starts, pick the note, slide up or down to the correct fret and continue the lick. You need to slide as quickly as possible so that it sounds like you're playing the lick with the usual timing, but with a special emphasis on the first note. If you have the tape for this book, listen carefully to this effect.

Here are a few examples. Notice that since the note you slide from is played very quickly, it often appears as a small *grace* note in the standard music notation.

The second way to use slides is to go for a note outside your current scale fingering. In this first lick, you're sliding into the 5th (D) in the key of G, on the seventh fret of the third string. Make the first slide from the fifth fret up to the seventh fret, and the remaining slides from the sixth fret to the seventh. There is also a slide back from the seventh fret to the fifth fret on the third string. Make sure you still hear both of the notes for their full value.

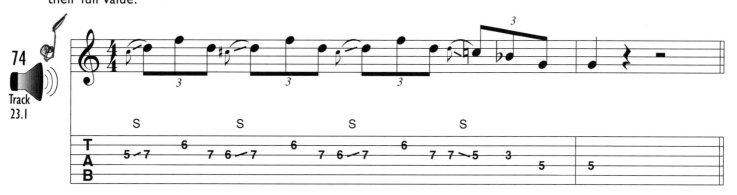

There are two different slides in this next one. First, a series of one-fret slides up to the major 3rd (B) in the key of G, at the seventh fret on the first string. Then at the end, a two-fret slide into the root (G) at the eighth fret on the second string.

This last one involves sliding on two strings at once. It's a similar to a lick that Stevie Ray Vaughn used all the time in open E, and it works further up the fretboard as well. All the slides are one fret—from the sixth to the seventh fret on the third string, and from the fifth to the sixth fret on the second string simultaneously.

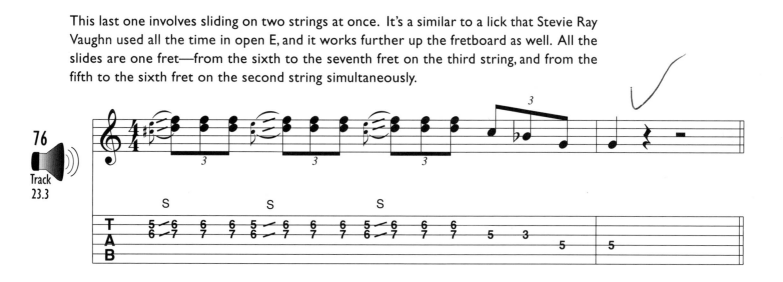

BENDING

There are two kinds of people in the world: people who bend strings, and people who don't. B.B. King bends. Albert Collins, Freddie King and Stevie Ray Vaughn were all serious benders. Albert King's whole life was one big bend.

Sometimes you can catch a jazz guy doing a bend. Not a very *big* bend—a tasteful little jazzy bend.

Segovia did not bend.

Bending is raising the pitch of a fretted note by pushing or pulling the string across the fretboard while keeping it pressed to the fretboard enough for it to still sound.

HALF STEP BENDS

A half step bend raises the pitch of a fretted note until it sounds the same as the note one fret above. We'll begin by bending from the 4th degree of the G Minor pentatonic scale on the third string.

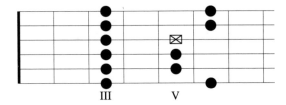

⊠ = bend this note

Starting from C on the fifth fret of the third string, bend until it sounds like a D♭—as if you just went from the fifth to the sixth fret on the G string. This is notated in the music or TAB as an arrow with a "1/2" over it. In the music the note that you're bending from is in smaller print (a *grace* note). In the TAB only the fret you're bending from is indicated.

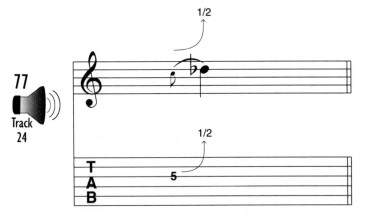

77
Track
24

As you practice bending, fret and play the note you're bending *to* first, to have the sound of the note you want to reach in your ear, before you actually do the bend.

Keep any fingers you can on the string behind the finger doing the bending to help push or pull the string. For example, if you're bending with your third finger from the fifth fret, have your second finger at the fourth fret and your first finger at the third fret on the same string and push with all three together to make the bend. Try not to bunch up your fingers. Use one finger per fret.

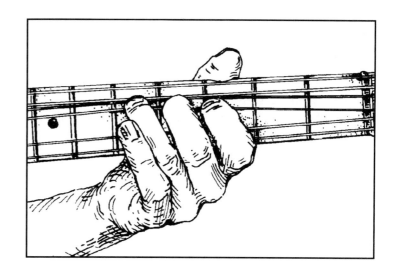

LICKS WITH HALF STEP BENDS

These licks in the G Minor pentatonic scale all use half step bends to incorporate D$^\flat$, the $^\flat$5 degree of the scale. This note does not belong to the minor pentatonic scale but blues players use it often.

WHOLE STEP BENDS

The 4th scale degree can also be bent a whole step, up to the 5th degree. The ♭3 on the first string can be bent a whole step up to the 4th. And the ♭7 on the second string can be bent a whole step up to the root.

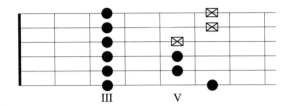

One of the best ways to check if you're bending the right distance is to work on the classic T-Bone Walker unison licks. (If you think they sound a lot like the classic Chuck Berry unison licks, you're right.)

81
Track 26.1

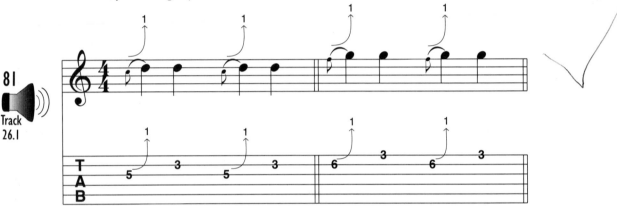

REVERSE BENDS

A *reverse bend* consists of *unbending* a note. The simplest way to do a reverse bend is to let a note you've just bent ring out as you unbend it. This is indicated in the music or TAB with a descending arrow. In the TAB, the fret on which you began the upward bend is shown in parentheses at the end of the reverse bend.

82
Track 26.2

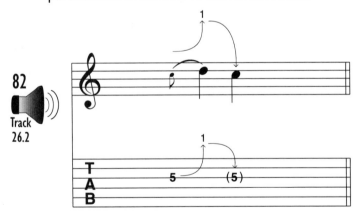

PREBENDS

Another way to do a reverse bend is to *prebend* a note. Raise the note without playing it, then hit the bent note and release it. This is indicated in the music and TAB with a vertical arrow for the prebent note, followed by a reverse bend.

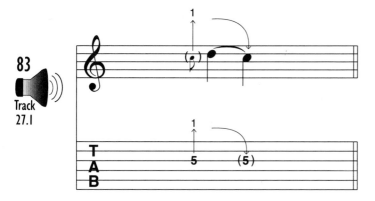

These examples all include reverse bends on various strings, as well as regular bends.

Here are six licks in the styles of some great blues guitarists. You will find regular bends and both kinds of reverse bends, too.

T - Bone Walker style. *Choke* the first bend in measure two (C to D) by releasing your finger as soon as you've made the bend.

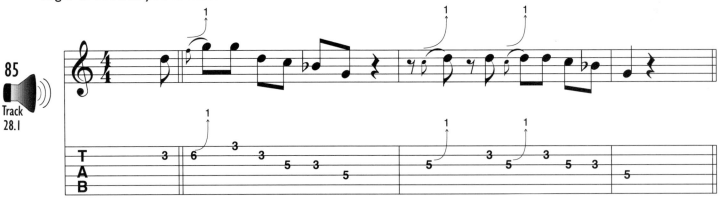

In the style of B.B. King

Albert King style

Albert Collins style

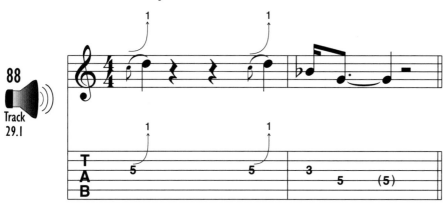

In the style of Michael Bloomfield

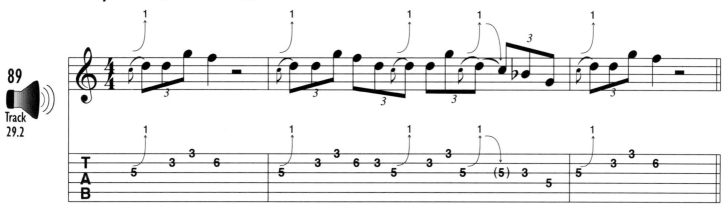

Just like Duane Allman

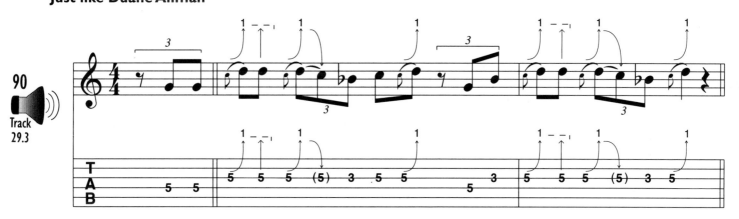

VIBRATO

Vibrato is the inflection you put on a note as you sustain it for any length of time. It sounds similar to what a singer does on long or held-out notes. Creating vibrato on the guitar is like doing a series of rapid-fire bends and releases that barely change the pitch of the string. Like bending, you can do vibrato by either pushing or pulling the string, and it helps to keep all available fingers on the string to help move it back and forth.

It's important for your vibrato to feel smooth and controlled, rather than tight or jittery, regardless of the tempo or feel of the song. These exercises will warm up your hand and get you playing evenly and with control.

Begin by playing half notes. Play a note, bend it just slightly sharp, return it to pitch, and raise it one more time.

91
Track 30.1

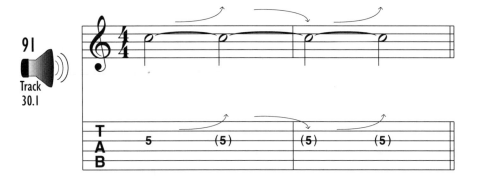

Repeat this several times in a row without pause at a set tempo. Then do quarter notes, still only picking once every two bars. The motion of bending and releasing the string should be enough to keep the note sustaining.

92
Track 30.2

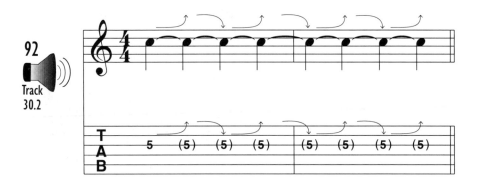

Move through eighth notes and sixteenth notes this way as well, at which point you can begin increasing the overall tempo too.

It is important that you always push or pull in only one direction, or your vibrato will sound inconsistant and strange. If you imagine the unbent string as "center," your vibrato should resemble this:

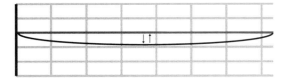

or this:

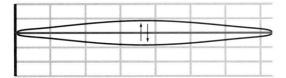

but not this:

B.B. King

Try playing this solo with vibrato as indicated by the symbol 〰. This example incorporates plenty of hammer-ons, pull-offs and bends as well. Notice that you frequently use vibrato on a note that has already been bent. This makes it sing as you "hold it up." To develop this sound further, go through the initial vibrato exercises using exclusively bent notes as your starting point.

CHAPTER 6

Rhythm Guitar Styles

As a rhythm guitarist, you can be an essential part of a band's sound. You can drive it forward or color it with an infinite variety of moods. Being a solid rhythm player is also a good way to make friends at jam sessions. You may spend more time on stage than someone else who solos great but can't hold down a groove for a singer.

With a good approach, playing rhythm guitar can be one of the most creative aspects of playing the blues. Every style of the blues has its own vocabulary of rhythm guitar licks; its own angle. Part of the fun of playing good backup at a gig is understanding these styles and working with them, instead of viewing the night as one three-hour long shuffle in A. Even if it is.

MUDDY WATERS—VAMPS

Muddy Waters fused the Mississippi country blues of his youth with electricity and the energy of a full band. This created and defined Chicago blues in the years after World War II. One strong characteristic of his sound was the *vamp*, which is a two-bar figure that can be repeated indefinitely.

These vamps often serve as the I chord in a twelve-bar blues.

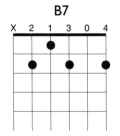

By now, you are familiar with the E7 and A7 chords. Here is a typical B7 voicing.

After working as a sideman to Muddy Waters in the '50s, Buddy Guy did some of his most influential work in the '60s with Junior Wells. In this collaboration, Buddy's rhythm style was based on single-note figures on the low strings. These *rhythm riffs* are similar to bass lines and can be moved around easily, like chord shapes. Use palm muting in this example.

There are many possible variations on this approach. Try taking these through an entire twelve-bar progression. Example 100 should be played with straight eighth notes, rather than with the usual shuffle feel.

With palm muting

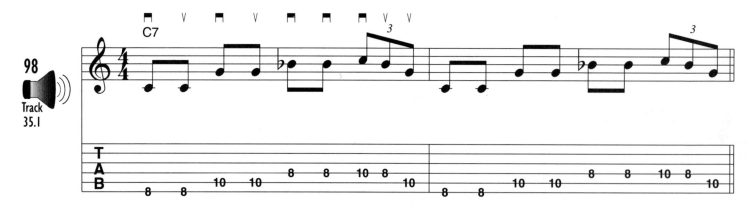

Slow Blues

Straight Eighths

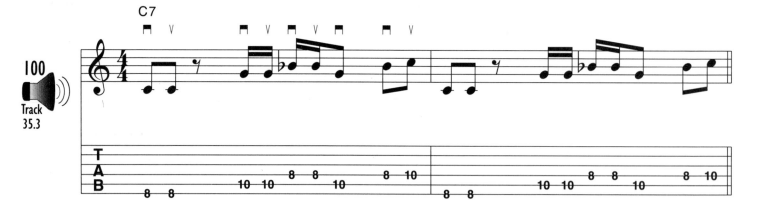

9TH CHORDS

Southwestern musicians have always made a habit of strolling back and forth across the line between blues and jazz, and from T-Bone Walker and Gatemouth Brown to Albert Collins and Stevie Ray Vaughn, the guitar players have been no exception. Often considered a jazz sound, *9th chords* are common in Texas blues. Refer to page 22 to review how 9th chords are constructed. Here are the two essential 9th chord voicings.

Two 9th chord voicings

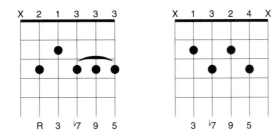

Notice that the chord on the right has no root. A voicing without a root works as long as there is another instrument playing the root of the chord.

9th chords create a whole new set of possibilities for the shuffle. Here are two shuffle patterns for a D9 chord.

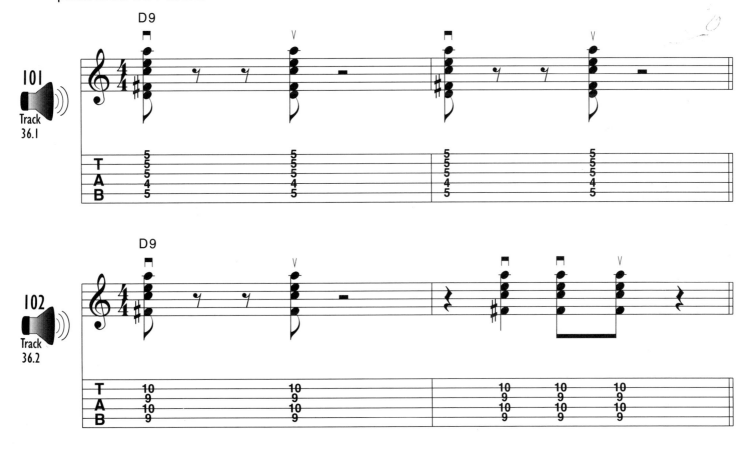

SLIDING CHORDS

Sliding the top three notes of a 9th chord up two frets and back creates another character-istically Texan sound. For the voicing with the root on the fifth string, slide just your ring finger up the strings and back, being sure to lift your index and middle fingers. For the rootless voicing, be sure to lift your index finger. If you slide the whole chord up, it will sound pretty weird. Here are three examples of these slides incorporated into a shuffle rhythm.

12/8 TIME

It is easier to think of a slow blues in the 12/8 time signature than in 4/4. You actually still have four beats, but every beat is subdivided into three little beats. Here are two rhythmic figures for a slow blues in 12/8.

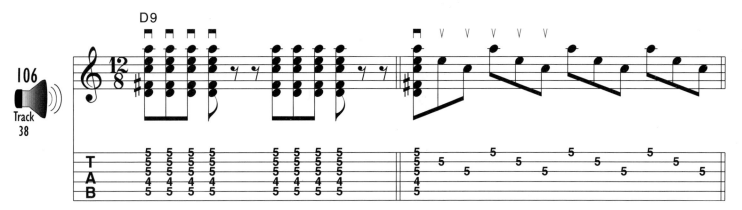

CHROMATIC MOTION

Chromatic motion means moving by half step. It is very common, especially in a slow blues, to move into a chord chromatically. Start one or more half steps above or below and move stepwise to the new chord on the downbeat of the next measure. There are five basic patterns for doing this.

Five Basic Patterns for Chromatic Motion

A) Start a half step above and move down.
B) Start a half step below and move up.
C) Start two half steps above and move down.
D) Start two half steps below and move up.
E) Play a half step above, then a half step below, then move up to the root.

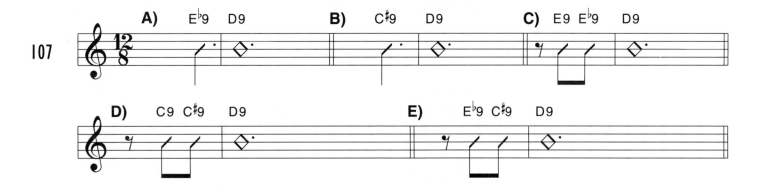

Finally, here is a complete chorus of slow blues using 9th chords and chromatic motion in 12/8 time. In the last four measures, use the rootless voicing from page 67 for everything except for the D9 chords. This includes the B♭9 in the eighth measure.

T - Bone Walker

For a basic minor blues, just substitute minor or minor 7th chords for the 7th chords in a standard twelve-bar form. Here are some chord voicings that work well for minor blues.

Minor

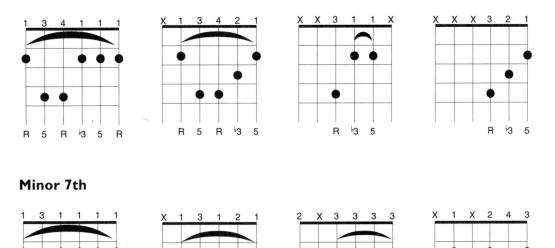

Minor 7th

Otis Rush ("All Your Love," "Double Trouble"), Buddy Guy ("One Room Country Shack"), Magic Sam ("I Just Got to Know") and others have recorded great slow blues tunes in minor keys. The approach is similar to slow blues in a major key—use chromatic chord motion and 12/8 time, as in the next example.

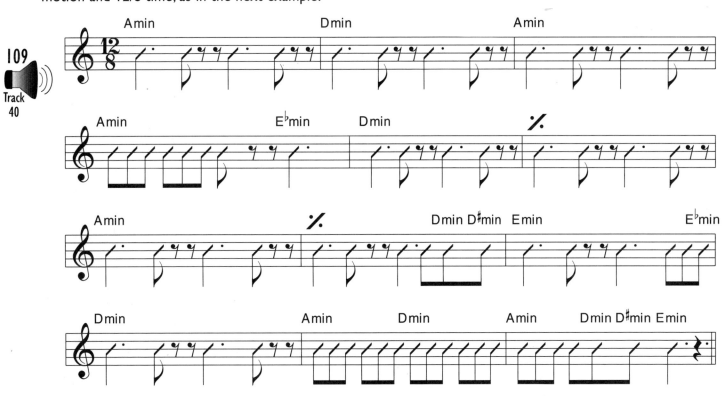

Up-tempo minor blues are commonly played with a straight-eighths feel—there are no swing eighth notes, and so there is no shuffle feel. B.B. King ("Help the Poor," "The Thrill is Gone"), Jimmy Johnson ("Serves Me Right to Suffer," "Heap See") and Robert Cray (just about everything) have all recorded minor blues tunes with rhythms taken from Latin, R&B and straight pop styles. Here are two up-tempo minor blues progressions. Notice that not *all* of the chords are minor. Remember to play the eighth notes without a shuffle feel.

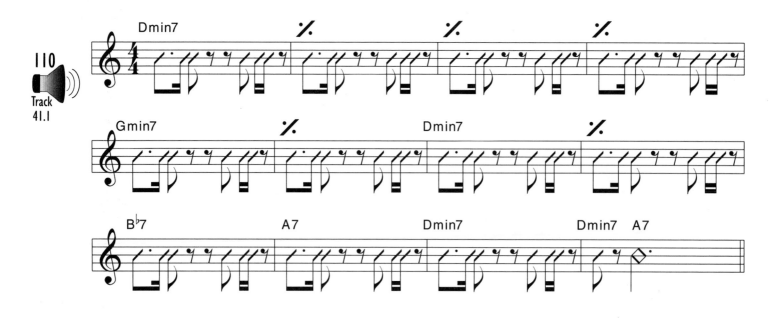

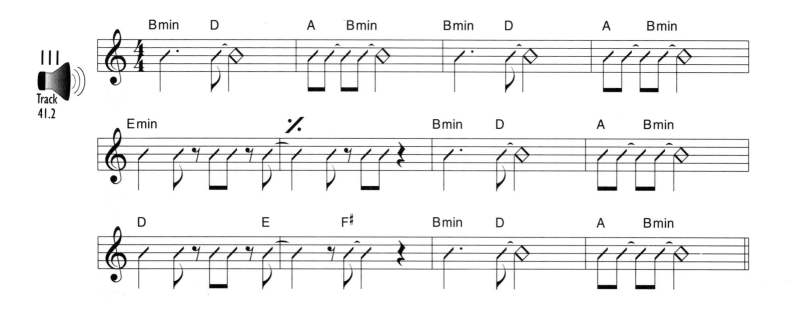

CHAPTER 7

Intros, Turnarounds and Endings

Right. So you're working on your phrasing. You're becoming more tasteful by the day. Your 9th chords are coming along and you've got that bar chord shuffle thing happening.. So you sit down with another guitar player and immediately run into problems...

"Whattya wanna play?"

"Well...you sing?"

"Nope. You?"

"Yeah, but I don't know any lyrics."

"Alright, what key should we play in?"

"I don't know. What kind of groove is it?"

"Just count it off. I'll come in."

"We gonna start on the I or take it from the turnaround?"

"All the way from the first V chord. Is this a regular I, IV, V?"

"Yeah, with a IV in the second bar, turnaround goes back up to a V at the end."

"Alright. I'm ready. Let's go."

"Okay, a-one, a-two, a-....Wait a second, how are we gonna end this thing?"

And so it goes.

Fortunately, unlike knowing which is the right fork to use for dessert, counting off tunes and communicating chord changes to other musicians are social skills nearly all of us can acquire with a little practice. If you are still shaky on the Roman numeral names for the chords (I, IV, V, etc.) go back and review the diatonic harmony section of Chapter 2.

Intros and endings are often based on turnarounds, so we will deal with those first.

TURNAROUNDS

The *turnaround* is the last four measures of a twelve-bar blues—from the beginning of the V chord in the ninth measure until the end of the twelfth measure. There may also be particular *turnaround licks* that are played in the last two measures, as part of the overall chord progression turnaround.

The simplest turnaround is to play through the progression as you normally would until the last measure. Then emphasize the V chord by dropping the first eighth note of the measure and playing the chord with no embellishments. Try left hand muting, too.

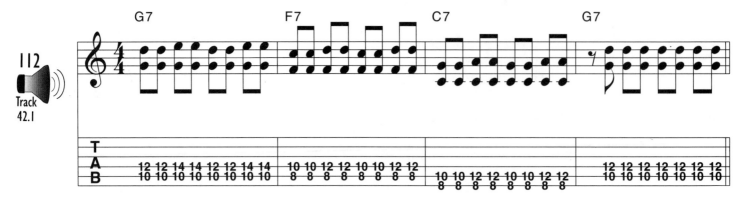

A slightly more suave and sophisticated ending involves playing normally through the down-beat of the twelfth measure, then coming into the V chord from a half step above, or the ♭VI chord, using 9th chords. Use palm muting for this example.

This kind of ending lends itself particularly well to including turnaround licks. This is demonstrated in the following four examples. Play normally through the downbeat of the second-to-last measure, then throw in one of these vintage phrases. The first two are descending lines, incorporated into a standard shuffle pattern. The second two are ascending lines incorporated into a Buddy Guy-style rhythm part. Use left hand muting in Examples 114 and 115, and palm muting in Examples 116 and 117.

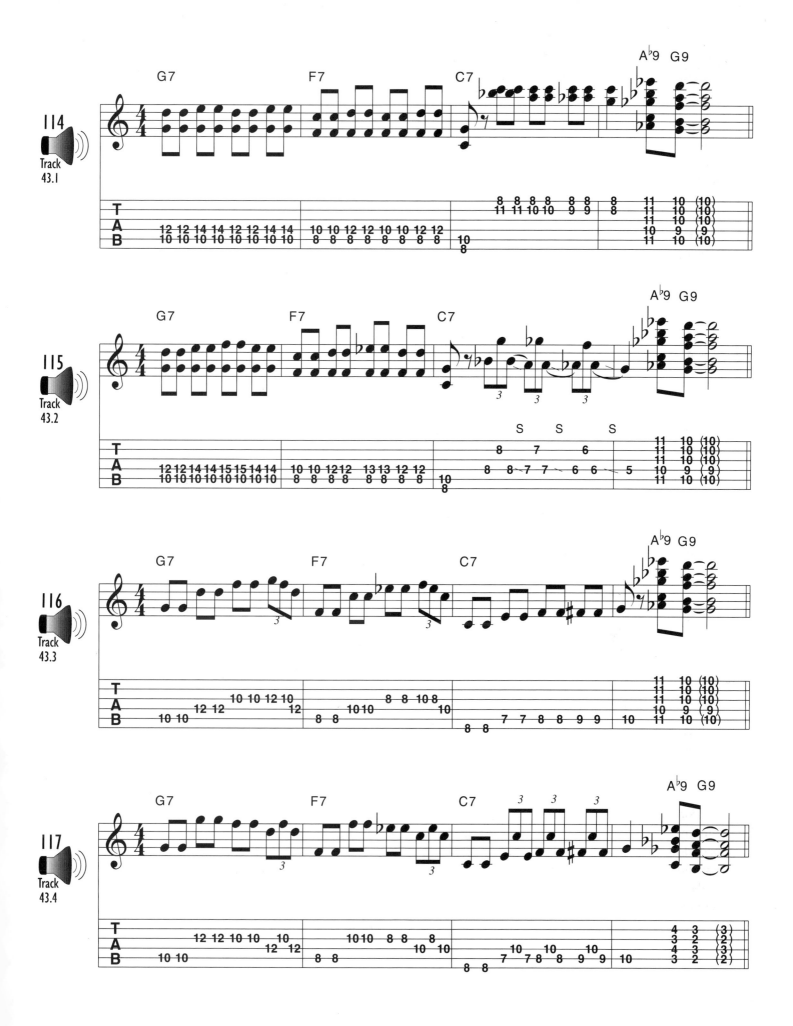

An *intro* is a short phrase played at the beginning of a song. The simplest intro is to begin a tune from the turnaround. Everybody just begins playing from the V chord in the ninth measure and the song "begins" after four measures, when you come around to the beginning of the twelve-bar form.

Next, you might take a particular chord-based riff and move it through all three chords of the turnaround, ending on a descending turnaround lick. Read about the slashed grace notes on the bottom of page 78.

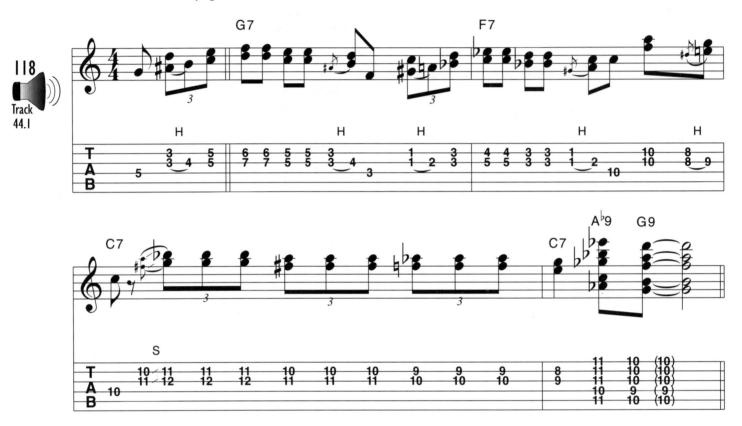

T - Bone Walker might open a slow blues with just a two measure intro, using only chords and chromatic motion.

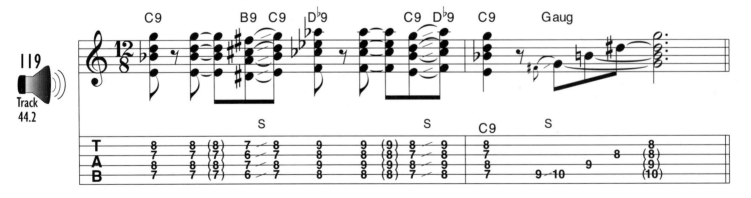

Here's a Muddy Waters-style intro for a slow blues. There is a slight variation in the chords. The first measure of the turnaround is half I chord, half V chord.

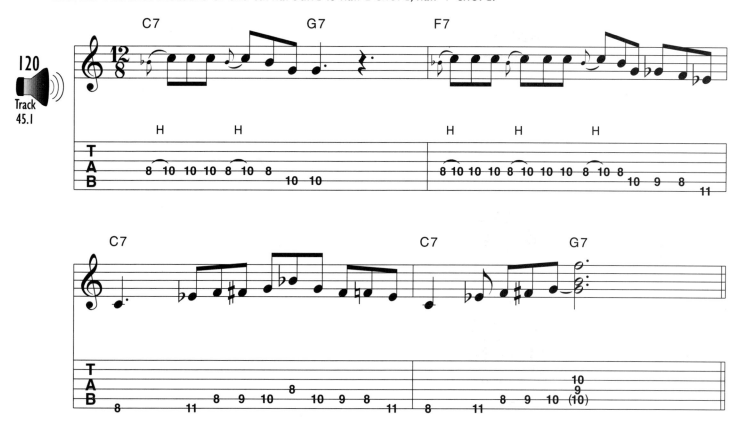

You can start a tune right at the beginning of the form using only *stop time.* As you learned in Chapter 3, stop time means playing short, percussive chord *hits.* Follow the chord progression, but leave space in between for a melody line.

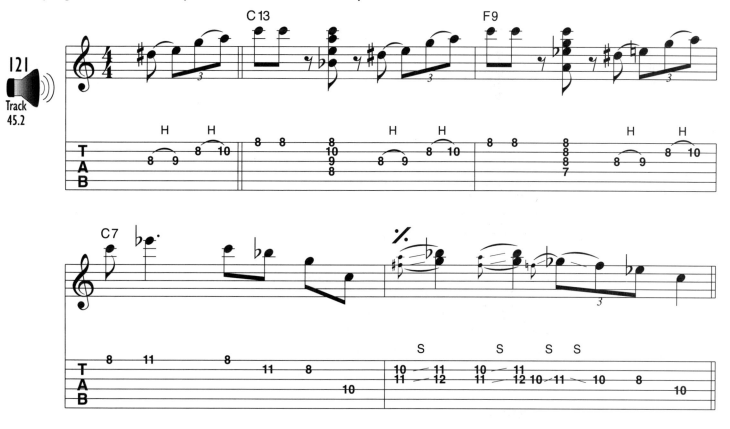

Some of the best endings are just introductions that end with half step chromatic motion to the I chord from the ♭II. Use left hand muting in Example 122.

122
Track 46.1

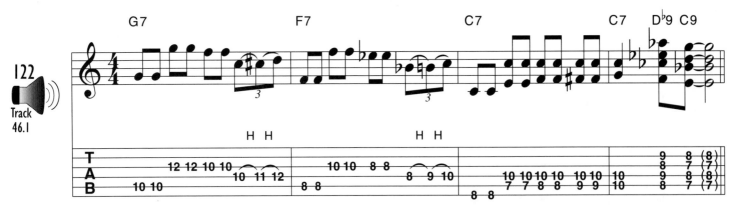

Go back and try making the rest of the turnaround examples into endings with a ♭II to I.

Another approach is to end with stop time. Play the final turnaround to the downbeat of measure eleven. Then, play a fill through the downbeat of measure twelve, and finish with the half step motion from ♭II to I.

123
Track 46.2

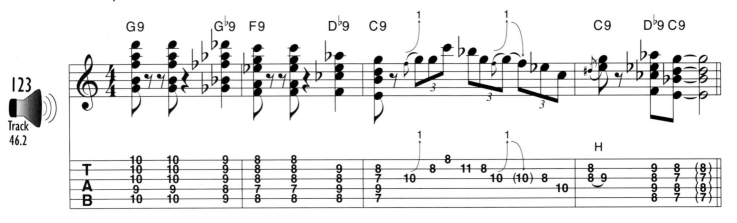

Examples 118 and 123 include a new kind of grace note.

For our purposes, the slash indicates that this note is played right on the beat, at the same time as the note above it. Since it's only a grace note, the hammer-on to the next note is executed immediately.

CHAPTER 8

Improvising

There's a reason people play pentatonic licks in the blues. They sound good. They sound like the blues. They're simple enough that you can spend less time learning them and more time learning how to use them—how to express yourself with them.

Still, everyone reaches a point when they feel bored and feel like they're playing the same things over and over again. This chapter will introduce you to some ways of getting more sounds and more ideas out of the basic scales. These examples show you how to use call-and-response techniques to alternate between the major and minor pentatonic scales, create space (using rests, a key to good phrasing) and mixing chords with single notes. This chapter will also cover how to combine the major and minor pentatonic scales.

ALTERNATING MAJOR AND MINOR PENTATONIC

Start off with a minor pentatonic phrase, then answer it with a major pentatonic phrase. Many great blues players seem to do this intuitively. If you play two phrases every four bars, it will have the sound of a singer (the minor phrase) being answered by an instrumental fill (the major phrase). See page 39 for moveable chord voicings that will work for these 7th chords.

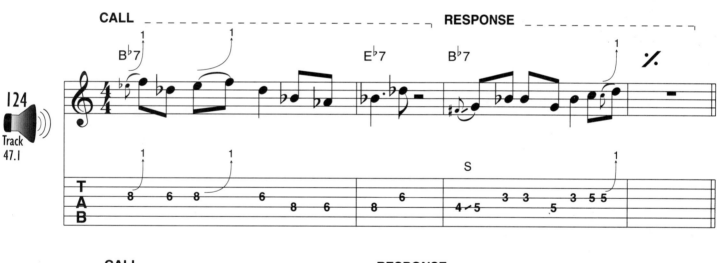

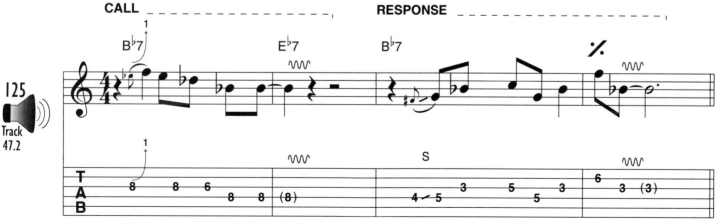

A powerful effect can be created by holding back the sound of the minor pentatonic. Play major pentatonic for the first eight measures of the chorus, then at the turnaround, switch to minor pentatonic. The contrast between scales will make even the usual minor licks sound fresh and give the turnaround the added impact it should have. Notice that in measure three there is a reverse bend, immediately followed by another bend, all on one pick. Also, in measure ten, a reverse bend is followed by a pull-off. Again, this is done on one pick.

Many of the swing licks favored by Texas style guitarists, as well as earlier B.B. King, involve borrowing the major 3rd and the major 6th from the major pentatonic scale and adding them to the minor pentatonic scale. Here is an example in B♭.

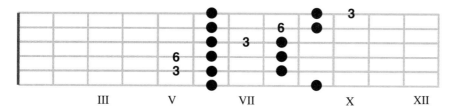

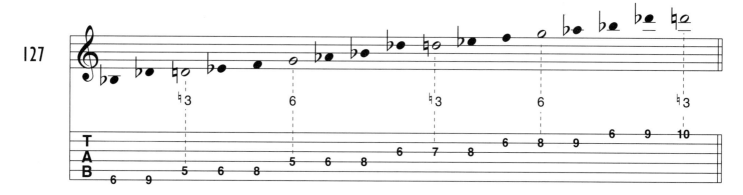

The major 6th sounds good on the I, IV or V chord. The major 3rd sounds best on the I chord but it clashes with the 7th of the IV7 chord. For example, in the key of A, the major 3rd of A is C♯, and the IV7 chord is D7, which has a C♮. The most effective use of the major 3rd is to include it when playing on the I chord, then change it back to the minor 3rd when playing on the IV chord. When this is done as part of a call and response, the result is characteristic of the Texas swing style.

ADDING MINOR PENTATONIC NOTES TO THE MAJOR PENTATONIC

As we discussed on page 81, if you play the major pentatonic scale as is, you are always playing the major 3rd of the scale against the 7th of the IV7 chord, creating a particularly uncool *dissonance*, or clash. (Some dissonances *are* cool. This isn't one of them.) You can solve this problem by borrowing notes from the minor pentatonic: the minor 3rd and the minor 7th.

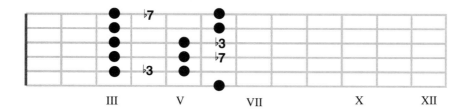

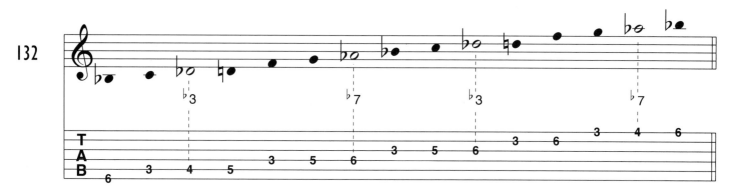

The minor 7ths sound best fretted normally, and work on I7, IV7 or V7, along with or instead of the major 6ths of the scale. The minor 3rds work three ways: fretting them normally, sliding into them, and bending to them.

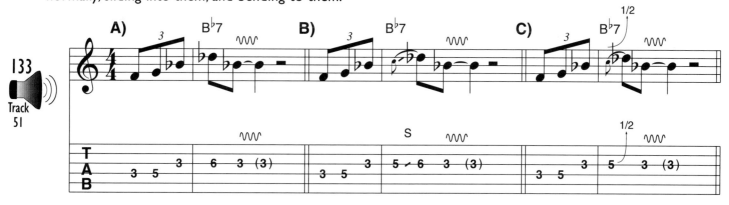

It is most effective to bend a whole step to the major 3rd over the I7 chord, then a half step to the minor 3rd over the IV7 chord. The minor 7th has the most impact in the fourth or eighth bar, as a lead-in to the IV7 or the V7 chord. This full-chorus example combines several of these techniques.

Chord hits add a new texture and set things up for some call-and-response phrasing, as well. In this first example, just 3rds and 7ths are used to outline the chords, and the licks are all in the minor pentatonic scale.

Examples 135 and 136 are both meant to be played without a rhythm guitarist. This will increase your ability to "hear" the chords of the progression go by as you play single notes. This is also a great technique for playing in a trio with only bass and drums. Also, it's time to get some practice reading music with a key signature. Since the next two examples are in B♭, they have two flats (B♭ and E♭) in the key signature. All the B and E notes are played flat unless marked otherwise. See page 17 for complete review of key signatures.

This example uses 9th chords approached from a half step above. In addition, the licks alternate between minor and major pentatonic.

Stevie Ray Vaughn

MINOR PENTATONIC

Learning the names of the notes in a scale of a particular key, and understanding what interval each scale degree is from the root, will greatly expand your range on the fingerboard. Here is an expanded version of the minor pentatonic scale we have been working with. The slide markings indicate when to shift positions, and the numbers show what fingers to use. This example is in the key of B♭.

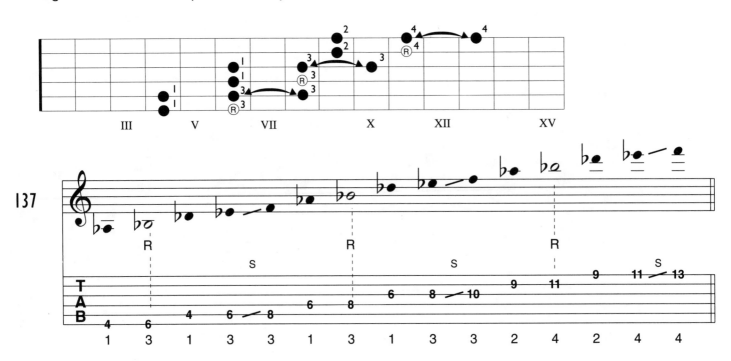

Keeping track of the root notes by always fretting them with your third finger or, on the high string, your fourth finger, will make the new areas of the fingerboard feel comfortable. Many of the licks you play in more familiar positions will come naturally. For example:

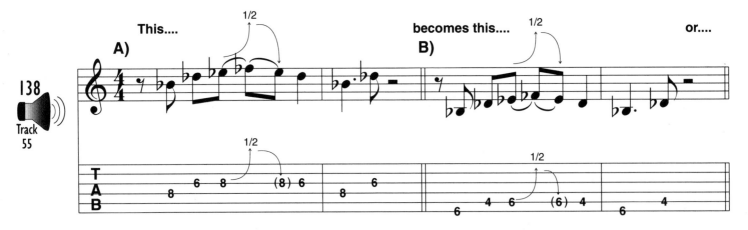

this.

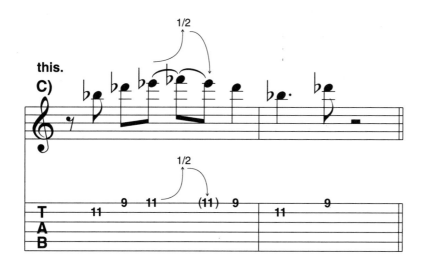

MAJOR PENTATONIC

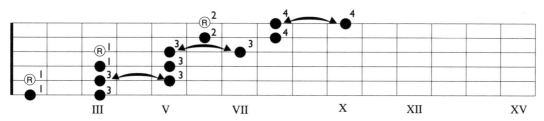

139

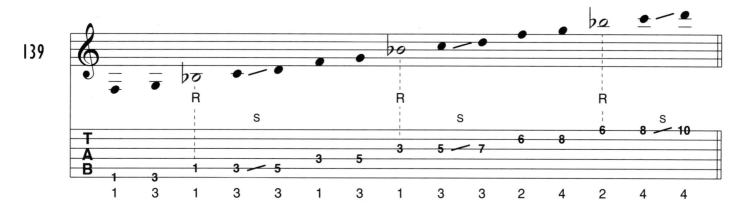

This doesn't look much like the old fingering. But, again, keeping track of the root notes can speed your orientation. This time fret the roots with your first finger, except on the first string, where you should use your second finger. Shifting where the slides indicate will help, too. Here are a few licks to illustrate how to transpose more familiar licks up or down an octave.

This.....   becomes this....   or this.

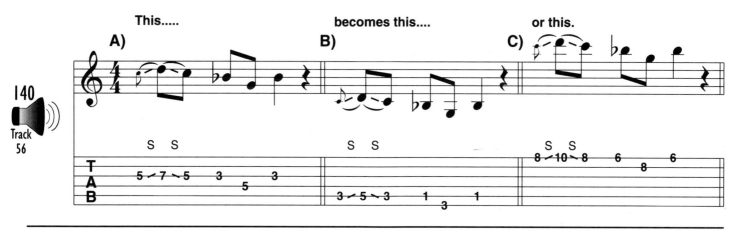

140

Track
56

CHAPTER 9

Practicing

These ideas are the results of my own efforts to find ways to learn that work for me, based on my own temperament, abilities and interests. I have developed many of the ideas in this book through teaching others. Several of the exercises, however, are based on how I teach myself and assimilate ideas I have received from fellow musicians, articles, teachers, and records.

These are suggestions, not rules (except for the section on metronomes).

SET GOALS

THE BIG PICTURE

Try to have as clear a picture as possible of what you want to be able to do. Clear, but general. For instance, "I want to be able to jam with other players," or, "I want to feel confident as a rhythm guitarist." Think about it in terms of where you'd like to be by this time next year, or by the time you finish working through this book.

SPECIFIC SKILLS

Next, break down that general picture into specific skills. If you want to be able to jam, that may mean knowing a handful of basic progressions and knowing you can play them in several keys without thinking about it too much. Or, maybe it means that you can find the right pentatonic positions for soloing and are even able to work in some licks pretty smoothly.

What would it mean to you to feel confident as a rhythm player? Maybe you need to learn once and for all how to hang on those first four measures of the I chord without losing track. Maybe you want to know a handful of blues "standards" and the original keys they were recorded in, and the kind of backup playing that sounds best for them—shuffle patterns, ninth chords, Chicago-style riffs, etc.

ORGANIZE YOUR TIME

SCHEDULING

If you can, put aside a small block of time each day that is yours for working on your playing. If possible, this should be at the same time each day. Note the use of the word *small*. You will do much better promising yourself twenty minutes with your guitar than promising yourself three hours. If it turns out you only have the patience for a little work that day, you won't feel that you let yourself down if you just work for the twenty minutes. On the other hand, once you actually sit down with your guitar (which is easier if it's "just for twenty minutes,") chances are something in your practice will intrigue you or annoy you enough that you'll start to get involved and suddenly wonder where the time went. At that point it's your choice whether to stop, knowing you spent the little time you had really well, or to feel extra dedicated and keep going for a little longer. (Sometimes I stop even if I'm really getting into things so that the next day I'll want to pick up where I left off.) Either way, you'll feel good about yourself and your practicing and end up looking forward to doing more the next time.

"LESSON DAYS"

Set up a "lesson" with yourself, especially if you don't have a private teacher. Choose a day of the week and make that your "lesson day." That's the day you sit down with whatever materials you're working on and assess, as honestly as you can, how you did over the past week. Then set out some new things to work on, probably some kind of continuation and advancement of the things you did the last week. Do it in writing.

If I'm working through a book of exercises, an instructional text, or a book of arrangements, I just jot down some notes in the margin of the current page. These notes will include the date and the various things I'm planning to work on that week, from that book and elsewhere. For instance, *"Pentatonic scales in F and B$^\flat$ with metronome, shuffle chorus on pg. 65, try and learn 3 licks off the Mike Bloomfield tune on side 2."* Some people keep a notebook or a music notebook—it doesn't matter. But keeping it in writing and doing it on a particular day will help you set reasonable goals. Gradually you will learn what you can expect from yourself in a week. When you only have a week to learn something, it seems like every day counts (which is true). But there's a difference between practicing every day because that's what Joe Shred says he did to get cool, and practicing every day because you are motivated to play well. Also, if you *do* miss a day here and there, who cares? As long as the general flow of things goes along, it's no tragedy. It's just like forgetting to eat lunch—your body catches up at dinner.

BALANCE

When you make your plans for the week, give yourself a variety of things to do. You need to work on different skills, giving your hands and brain a shift of gears within each practice session. Try to balance working on **physical technique**, **mental technique**, and **repertoire**. For example, practicing a scale in a particular pattern with the metronome for accuracy and precision strengthens your fingers and hands. That's physical technique—developing your ability to react quickly and execute your ideas. Taking a chord progression at a comfortable tempo and playing it in every key is more of a workout for your brain. You have to think about how the chords relate to each other, where to find the first chord of each new key on the fingerboard, and so on. Learning songs from a book, off of a record, from a teacher or from another musician helps you increase your repertoire of songs. While all three types of practice involve aspects of each other, and reinforce each other too, it helps to work on them separately. It allows you to focus on one skill at a time when you work.

IMPROVISATION

Improvising may be the hardest thing to practice because it's so easy to just go off on a tangent from what you need to work on, or just playyour licks over and over. Do your technical workout first when you practice, and when you do begin your improvising, try and work with some of the routines given in Chapter 8 for creating contrast. Be as specific as possible about what you are actually practicing. Switching every four bars from major to minor pentatonic and back again is a tangible guideline, for instance. If you tape yourself you will know if you're getting it or not.

METRONOMES, DRUM MACHINES, AND PRACTICE TAPES/CDS

METRONOMES AND DRUM MACHINES

Okay, who hates the metronome? Let's see some hands...

Believe it or not, the dreaded metronome is actually a great practice tool when used well. *Here are some rules you should follow:*

Use it to confirm the tempo you need to play every note in an exercise confidently, accurately and in good rhythm. Then begin to increase the tempo, one or two settings at a time, maximum. The metronome is just a tool to measure, establish and maintain solid practice tempos. It will also help you pace yourself as you train for faster tempos. People only develop metronome trauma when they set the metronome *faster* than they are able to play an exercise and attempt to "catch up."

Set it so one click equals a quarter note and it clicks on every beat. When you're used to that, set it twice as slow and try to hear it as only the second and fourth beats, like a snare drum backbeat. Use it when you practice scales, chord progressions, switching chords, phrases, complete solos and tunes.

Use the metronome as much as you can to practice. If you have a drum machine, you can use that instead, with a simple click or a basic groove. Everything needs to be in time eventually, and if you can make playing with the metronome second nature, it will help your ability to count off a tune, count measures and play with other people.

PRACTICE TAPES AND CD'S

Practice tapes and CDs can help too, especially for working on your improvising. I used to spend hours taping myself playing I-IV-V on a little tape recorder and then playing over it (yeah, my family loved listening to *that!*). Now you can get recordings of a whole band playing rhythm tracks for you to solo over. You can even use them to practice your scales and patterns *first* to hear how they sound over the chords, and *then* go into your soloing. This is a good way to work on your phrasing and solo development because the solid beat is there, just like with the metronome, but you also hear the chords changing underneath. The National Guitar Workshop and Alfred have released *Stand Alone Blues* and *Stand Alone Blues and Beyond* play-along tapes and CDs (which I'd probably recommend even without my editor's sordid kickback offer involving free advance copies for me and a crate of Beluga caviar for my cat). Jamey Aebersold has a series of recordings aimed at jazz players, of which Volumes 24 (major and minor vamps in every key) and 42 (jazz-style blues in every key) should be of interest to blues players.

VARY YOUR SOURCES

RECORDINGS

There is a great deal you can learn from recordings. Obviously, there's the note-for-note approach. But don't stress if you can't get a whole solo down. In fact, try starting with the fills. They're short, well-defined, and it's easy to hear where they begin and end. In addition, try to catch some of the rhythm playing. Listen to the hits, the rhythms and the groove. What's the bass player doing? What about the drummer? Listen to the pianist and the harmonica player. What's the form of the song? What kind of intro does it have? What's the order of verses and solos? Which instruments do fills as a way of keeping things interesting and varied in each verse?

Every time you go back and listen to certain records you will hear something you didn't notice before. You may spend months listening to the lead playing on a record without thinking about it. Then one day you might suddenly realize that you want to learn some new songs, and go to that album. Or, your band may want to play "Frosty" by Albert Collins and you need to learn the melody. Or maybe you want to learn some New Orleans rhythms, so you decide to get hold of some Professor Longhair or the Meters. Sooner or later you'll start to hear music everywhere—not just in guitar playing—and it will give you all kinds of ideas for things to try on the guitar.

OTHER SOURCES

Any time you hear live music, attend a seminar or master class, take a private lesson with a different teacher, read a guitar magazine, or just sit down and play with another musician, you can take something from it that grabs you and bring it into your practice routine. Make some notes about what it is you saw or learned and try to go through the steps of learning it or learning about it. For example, if you learn a new chord voicing, practice switching to and from it. Try putting it into a tune you know well and one that you're still working on.

Use a magazine transcription as part of your work for one week as a break from this or other books.

Spend some time on a style outside your favorite. It's all guitar, and besides giving you new ideas and a different perspective, you can bring something different back into your usual collection of licks and grooves.

OUTSIDE THE PRACTICE ROOM

"TAPE DOESN'T LIE"

Every time you get to jam, perform or "sit in" is a chance to see how well you do "in the real world." Hopefully you'll have a great time, but even if you fall on your behind, you will wake up the next morning and know exactly what needs work. I've heard tapes of myself playing live that just made me cringe. But, as recording engineers are fond of pointing out, "tape doesn't lie" and you can learn a great deal by hearing yourself.

If you can, bring a little tape recorder to your gigs and have a friend "bootleg" the show. Studio or home recording is great too, if you have access to the equipment. Even taping yourself jamming with another guitar player is valuable. Listen to both your lead and rhythm playing carefully. You'll hear your phrasing, tone, sense of rhythm and ideas with a more objective ear. Maybe those solos were longer than you thought!

COMPETITION, HEALTHY AND OTHERWISE

You can learn a great deal from your fellow musicians, and as you improve, there will be things you can show them too. Wanting to be as good as you can be is very motivating. Wanting to blow people away is also motivating, but you have to ask yourself what it means. Some musicians always play really fast and as loud as they can get away with. They always seem to be busy jamming (even if they're not entirely welcome). Often, they are like people who talk too much. They're mostly trying to prove to themselves that they're cool—that everything's okay. The truly confident player who knows his or her own abilities and limitations can lay back, musically and personally, and wait for the right opportunity to make a real statement.

INDIVIDUALITY

How you practice, develop, and perform are as personal as who you are. This means you are entitled to your individuality. As long as you understand that musicianship is a healthy balance of technical, mental, emotional and creative skills, you should proceed at your own pace and set your own terms as a musician. Teachers and books are there to help you, and often an experienced teacher or older musician may have insights into your path of development that you can't see yourself. It is up to you whether you trust that person enough to invest the time and hard work for something that may, or may not, make sense to you.

It is ultimately your choice to decide what to work on and pursue. Cultivate your own judgement and gut feelings. When you listen to something new, you *know* if it moves you or not. Everything new to you deserves the benefit of the doubt, so if you can't stand something, put it on the back burner and listen again in six months or a year. Then, if you still can't live with it, don't. Don't be intimidated that "this is so-and-so, you know, the 1957 sessions cut out in the parking lot with a console powered by the cigarette lighter in Leonard Chess' Packard." Respond to the playing, not merely the story surrounding it. No two people are the same. How on earth could any two people practice the exact same way, like the exact same records, or play the exact same way?

Music is for individuals. Be one.

Ronnie Earl

PHOTO · COURTESY RONNIE EARL